BLAST OPEN BIG DOORS

How to Prospect Fortune 1000 Companies

Ignite your sales

www.gunpowderbusiness.com

"I could not put this book down! I thought I knew all I needed to know about sales, but Christine's strategies raised the bar to a whole new level."
Karen Brunger, Director, International Image Institute Inc.

"Simply brilliant! Every page of "Blast Open Big Doors" is chock full of practical, usable ideas to create an avalanche of profitable, new meetings with high level decision makers. Christine's new book isn't just for sales professionals alone, but any executive, entrepreneur or business owner who wants to quickly expand their client base in a challenging economy. I highly recommend this powerful, insider blueprint for creating exciting breakthroughs in your sales results!"
Paul Low, Business Growth Catalyst

"Read it – loved it ... the material makes a lot of sense and it should be extremely appealing to anyone in sales, sales management, business development."
Horst Schmidt, Director, SMB Sales, Unity Telecom

"Many talk about opening C-level doors, Christine does it -- and once the door is open, she knows how to close multi-million dollar deals."
Toby Ward, President, Prescient Digital Media

"Her well-crafted book will open your eyes to no-nonsense tactics to make your business more successful."
Howard Breen, Chairman Emeritus, MacLAREN McCANN

"We all encounter things we need to do, or conversations we need to have, but dread, and your program made us all less willing to take 'No' for an answer...even from ourselves."
Lorraine Greey

"Christine's innovative approach to customer acquisition has presented us with opportunities that our competition could only dream about."
Robert Logan, Senior Vice President of Sales, Camilion Solutions Inc.

"Blast Open Big Doors" workshop. I have been to many of these types of sessions and was very impressed with Christine as a Keynote Speaker and as a Workshop Facilitator. I walked away motivated and with actionable take-a ways to put what I had learned into practice."
Grail Nobel, President, Yellow House Events

"Christine is a passionate and professional keynote speaker. Her topic of prospecting and landing clients has a very wide appeal, and she has a tremendous wealth of knowledge on the subject. We all want to land more and bigger clients, and Christine is a proven resource to help achieve those results."
Josh Linkner, Founder & Chairman, ePrize

"We used Gunpowder to facilitate opening doors for our business development team. They were able to secure executive-level meetings we otherwise would not have been able to obtain."
Michael Zahra, President, Staples Advantage Canada

"There's no question that we've been able to build our market share faster with Gunpowder's help. When we started, we had absolutely no presence in the U.S. Universities market. Now we're one of the top three suppliers – and the likelihood is that we wouldn't have been able to get there without Gunpowder."

Ted Madden, COO, Comtext Systems, IntelliResponse Systems Inc.

"Christine's wealth of experience and interesting parodies leave you hanging from her every word. Then sadly before you know it, time has flown by and you are left wishing you could rewind the clock to hear more!"

Colette Hustwick, Jones DesLauriers Insurance Management Inc

"I have watched in awe for the past two decades as Christine kicked open one Presidential door after another. Her ideas are powerful. If you want to go hunting for elephants, you better take along the "Gunpowder"!"

Gregory Cleary, Sales Coach, Action Learning Corporation

"Getting to the right person is critical and Gunpowder proved time and time again that they could deliver. Having used Gunpowder in Canada I was only too pleased to recommend them to our colleagues in the USA and later on my return to Europe to ensure that we signed them up to assist our strategic sales teams across Europe."

Peter Ventress, Chief Executive, Davis Service Group Plc,
Former President, Staples International

"Christine has an ability to connect to her audience with a mixture of information and examples laced with humour. She shares practical ideas and proven success stories to inform and motivate her audience."

Kelly Burnett, The Calyx Group

"I have had the privilege to hear Christine's speak on several occasions. Each time I have come away inspired with new ideas and motivated to reach even higher. She draws deeply from her many years of experience and gives you the inside secrets on how to be more successful in today's business world. Spending time with Christine is always profitable."

Alexi Helligar, Sr. Information Architect Mojeaix IT Solutions

"Her style is entertaining, as her sense of humour is evident in the presentations as she enlivens and entertains, she gets her message across."

James Phillipson, Principal, Mastermind Solutions Inc.

"At first I was confused as to why the Gunpowder team needed to know so much about our value proposition, just to set an appointment. Once I ran my first appointment it was abundantly clear! We were meeting the true decision maker and he knew what we came to discuss. That one appointment turned into $6MM in new business."

Deb Trout, Director, Business Development,
Direct Mail Organization, Staples, Inc.

"For an insightful and thoughtful approach to not only growing your business, but also developing a stronger leadership style, look no further than 'Blast Open Big Doors!'"

Karen Windsor, WINDSORCommunications

To order additional copies of this title: www.gunpowderbusiness.com; www.apple.com in the iBooks store; www.amazon.com

Phone: 416-823-0456   e-mail: caquin@gunpowderbusiness.com

Cover and page design by Jerry Dorris of www.authorsupport.com

Cover and Interior Images: ThinkStock.com

Library and Archives Canada Cataloguing in Publication

Aquin Pope, Christine

Blast open big doors : how to prospect fortune 1000 companies / Christine Aquin Pope.

Issued also in electronic format.

ISBN 978-0-9867448-0-8

1. Telephone selling. 2. Sales meetings.

3. Sales management. I. Title.

HF5438.8.M4A98 2010 658.8'106 C2010-906746-0

Printed in Canada

About the Author

CHRISTINE AQUIN POPE

The founder and president of Gunpowderbusiness Development, Christine Aquin Pope is also a dynamic keynote speaker. With over 15 years of experience in sales and business development, Christine is an expert at designing sales processes that drive significant new revenues.

Christine developed a **Bulletproof prospecting system** that has opened over **19,000** big doors to the executive suites in leading corporations around the world—including Bank of America, Time Warner, and Procter & Gamble. Her research-based strategies have been proven effective across a number of industries, including technology, automotive components, hospitality, insurance, and banking. She specializes in helping salespeople and business owners with her proven methods for perfecting prospecting and accelerating sales, allowing them to **succeed without the fear of rejection**.

In her earlier career as a salesperson, she developed and sold over $45 million in products and services throughout North America and spearheaded significant business growth initiatives across a range of industries. Her vast experience on the front line has included selling complex software to package good and insurance companies, media space for Citytv, and interactive media campaigns to well-known brands, such as Delta Airlines, Aeroplan, Avon Inc., Tiffany & Co., and Holt Renfrew.

Based in Toronto, Christine ignites sales teams all over the globe with her inspiring, humourous keynote presentations and workshops.

www.gunpowderbusiness.com

Acknowledgements

This book is dedicated to those who died in the terrorist attacks of September 11, 2001.

These events touched my heart so profoundly that I decided to take a three month sabbatical from selling. Little did I know where that sabbatical would lead me. I flew with my mom and daughter to Maui, where I met a young man named Big Mike whose specialty was kite surfing. Big Mike was from Connecticut; he was building a home in Maui while working his Connecticut business from his lap top and cell phone. This inspired the thought: "How could I do that?" From this thought, Gunpowderbusiness was born.

Richard Yeni is an old friend. When I first began my new company, his sales manager hired me on the spot. Since then, Richard has since hired us four times, and without his support none of this would have ever started.

John Collins is another dear friend. His constant encouragement helped me overcome my fear, my internal demons, and made it possible for me to start my own business. John is our corporate lawyer; he makes sure our contracts are rock solid. I remember the day he was working up our first contract and he needed to register our business name. I looked down at my cup of tea—it was Gunpowder green tea—and I said, "John, what do you think about Gunpowderbusiness for our name?" Being a conservative lawyer, he told me he hated it; I knew I had a winner. We love our name, because we love blasting open big doors and igniting sales for our clients. (I think John likes it now, too.)

Great businesses are built with great clients, and this is the perfect place to thank some of ours. My gratitude goes out to the late Peter Herbert, who stood tall and said, "I want to be proactive and not be the last one invited to an RFP; I want to help prospects write the RFP!" (He did.) I am also grateful to Gregg Malmstrom and Lex Elkins, who challenged us to keep growing our team as they grew theirs. These two men stood by us through all the growing pains that accompany the launch of a new business. Everyone at Gunpowderbusiness thanks you!

I am also indebted to my editors, Brandon Yusuf Toropov, Diana Byron, Tamara Kronis and our proof reader Ruth McKay. Their enthusiasm about the material gave me the confidence to share this book with you, to start doing keynote talks, and to offer workshops that teach small business owners how to double their revenue.

A special thank you goes out to my daughter, Natasha, who was 10 years old when I started Gunpowderbusiness and who, in the early days, had to share her home with our business. I know it was not always easy coming home to house full of aggressive (and protective) sales people. She motivated me in so many ways that I get choked up just thinking about it. She is my inspiration for helping to make this world a better place. To my three stepsons, Alexander, Nicholas, and Henry—I love having you in my life. To my husband, Francis, with your love and constant humour I know I can reach all my dreams and then some! I love you all dearly.

Table of Contents

Preface

The profession of sales is tough; there's no doubt about it. The road to success is filled with confidence-shaking landmines: rejection, budget cuts, layoffs, and stress-inducing quotas. But this book is here to help, providing you with a road map to help you navigate around those landmines. The tactics I lay out in this book are based on one of my favourite sayings—"big doors turn on little hinges." The steps I'll show you are small, simple, and easy, but using them will enable you to take your business through any big door you like.

I wrote this book because booking great sales meetings is a skill that can double your revenue, and it's one you can learn. Time and time again I've watched good salespeople fail because they lacked to right tools; they didn't have a road map. I know I can prevent this failure, so I'm going to share with you our previously top-secret battle-tested strategies for connecting with the right decision makers. The Gunpowder Bulletproof Prospecting System will teach you to prospect for new business in the most effective way possible.

At Gunpowderbusiness, our mission is to equip you to achieve sales results beyond your expectations. We take ordinary salespeople, wrap a well-thought-out sales process around them, and turn them into extraordinary salespeople. We approach blasting open big doors like a strategic military operation. We do this because successfully targeting the doors of a Fortune 1000 company requires:

- precision.
- simple tactics that, when implemented together, are extremely powerful.
- discipline to ensure follow through and execution.

Winning an unfair share of the marketplace is the name of the game. That is the mission. By prospecting far more efficiently and effectively than most salespeople do, you will dramatically accelerate your sales cycle and complete your mission.

I like using military terminology in this program because I am showing people how to discipline their sales activities and how to set themselves up for success. This requires military-level discipline. I see far too many unprepared salespeople sent out to the front line, only to fail. This failure is unnecessary—if you are properly armed, you will be able to compete in today's global marketplace.

The marketplace is a battlefield, and Bulletproofing yourself with my simple prospecting strategies will protect you from injury on that battlefield. Bulletproofing yourself by taking the steps to prepare properly before launching your campaign will:

- protect you from rejection.
- prevent you from looking or feeling foolish.
- prepare you for every step of the prospecting process.
- give you a system of success you can easily follow.
- set you up to win more opportunities with decision makers.

It's a simple fact that if you become an expert at prospecting, you will double your sales.

A lot of good ideas appear on the following pages, but if they stay as ideas—if you never execute them—then you will have failed in your mission. Turning good ideas into habits will require effort on your part. It will require discipline. Think of yourself as a Navy SEAL. Are Navy SEALs impatient, stressed, or easily spooked by obstacles? Of course not! They're totally focused on the mission, and they're models of discipline and purpose—even when they have to revise their plans on the ground. If you develop the discipline to execute the tactics I'm about to share with you, you can win more than your share of the marketplace—just like I did, and just like our clients do. The results speak for themselves: hundreds of millions of dollars worth of sales every year for our clients.

The Gunpowder Bulletproof Prospecting System is tried, tested, and proven to accelerate the point at which you get to state your case to top-tier people and win a bigger piece of business than your competitors. To succeed with it, you must prepare yourself, do the right activities, and track your own work as you go. When you are properly prepared, you work from a solid foundation of confidence—you are Bulletproof.

I understand how tough it is out there; the world is changing, borders are falling, and you're facing strong competition from many different countries. I'd like to see North America continue to be a global leader, and I believe our advantage lies in our innovation and creativity. Using the Gunpowder Bulletproof Prospecting System will help you to stand out and compete in this global marketplace and take your business to a whole new level. Simply by following this prospecting system, anyone can capture a bigger piece of the global pie.

Happy hunting!
Christine Aquin Pope

Foreword

Let's face it, sales has always been a challenging profession. With the recent economic meltdown, it's become even tougher. But opportunities are still out there, you just need grit, determination, and a plan to access them. Christine Aquin Pope has that plan, and she's about to show you the techniques that will help you to blast open the big doors that stand between you and success. Your success will be a team effort—you provide the grit and determination, and Blast Open Big Doors will provide you with a bulletproof plan.

As a marketing executive for a software company that sells multi-million dollar enterprise solutions to financial services organizations, one of my biggest challenges was getting access to the C-suite. Our deals took months, even years, to close, and it was my job to fill the pipeline and get C-level meetings for our sales executives so they could establish a rapport with the decision makers and nurture those relationships to success. Christine and her Gunpowderbusiness team were instrumental in helping us get those critical C-level meetings; introducing us to some of the highest ranking executives in the financial services industry. Christine also helped transform our value proposition into a compelling conversation that her sales team, and the company's, could use to secure those meetings. Thanks to her process, there are multiple deals progressing through the pipeline, which will help the company meet its aggressive growth and revenue goals.

A sales veteran with over 15 years of experience, Christine now acts as a consultant for businesses that want to take their game to the next level. Her previously top-secret techniques are now available to you in this book. Entertaining, easy to read, and full of great information and strong examples, Blast Open Big Doors is sure to help you elevate your sales career.

I hope you find Christine's methods as successful as I have at accelerating growth.

Good luck.

Gwen Lannaman

Vice-President, Marketing

CHAPTER ONE

Welcome to Gunpowder's Bulletproof Prospecting System

"I will be allowed to fulfill my destiny!"
~ GENERAL GEORGE S. PATTON JR.

The marketplace is a battlefield, and my Bulletproof Prospecting System will help you to blast open big doors—behind which lie opportunities for explosive business growth. Over the last 15 years I have made a specialty of prospecting Fortune 1000 companies. With the world marketplace more accessible than ever, the time has never been better for your company to sell globally. The sales process I reveal in this book will allow you to complete your mission: winning more than your share of the marketplace.

Make no mistake, executing these tactics will require effort and discipline, but it will be worthwhile. Why? Freedom. I'm talking about financial freedom, freedom from fear, freedom of choice, freedom to make your own world a better place. The Gunpowder Bulletproof Prospecting System will set you on the path to freedom, however you choose to define it.

"The sad fact is that people are poor because they have not yet decided to be rich."
~ BRIAN TRACY

Many salespeople lack good training and good tools. It's a mistake I see all the time, with both large and small organizations. The sales executives just don't have the depth of knowledge they need to be successful. They often don't even have the basic sales tools they need to get that critical first meeting at the right level of decision making. I have seen and worked with some brilliant sales professionals who failed simply because they could not meet with enough well-placed people fast enough.

The Gunpowder Bulletproof Prospecting System will arm you with the training and tools you need to ensure that this doesn't happen to you.

You'll learn how to book high-level meetings quickly and efficiently. And that's the goal: meeting with enough well-placed people. This book identifies the key process for you. I have field-tested it in the real world. I know it works because, time and time again, I was the magic bullet salesperson who was brought in to save the day. I was able to use this system to take the pressure off myself. Now, after two decades of troubleshooting, I have built a book around this system...so you can use it to take the pressure off yourself.

HOW I GOT MY FIRST SET OF COMBAT BOOTS

The system came into being years ago. I was working in the research department at a company called Citytv when I was suddenly promoted into sales. At that time, Citytv was the third-largest television station in Canada, but television advertising was a relatively new medium for Canadian retailers. I was given a small base salary, a handful of existing clients, and a million-dollar quota. We had no sales kit; we had glossy one-sheet blurbs about our shows, such as Seinfeld. We sold 30-second advertising spots on these shows for $25,000 each. I remember looking at the Seinfeld one sheet. There was Jerry looking at me with that beautiful smile, however, he wasn't sharing the secrets of how to convince business owners to buy television spots. In fact, these one sheets had no real hard data on them, and I was left thinking, "How in the world do I get a retail owner in Toronto to drop 25 grand on one 30-second spot during a re-run—using this?"

Well, I had to figure it out; I had my big reason why: Natasha, my daughter. I was a single mother, and my family was counting on me. I had to develop my own materials. I had to learn how to develop a good prospect list. I had to figure out how to generate enough confidence to persuade clients to switch money from their newspaper and radio budgets, something that they knew worked for them, to a new medium—television. I did figure it out, and I had a ton of fun there for three years. The process I wrapped around myself to make it all work is what allowed me to succeed—it was the start of the Gunpowder Bulletproof Prospecting System.

I realize, of course, that I was lucky that Citytv had a good brand name, which made getting appointments relatively easy. Sometimes I was able to entice my clients to meet me at the television station. The lure of giving them a private tour went a long way to maximizing my selling time. Even with these advantages, though, it was still my job to set up and improve my own process.

LEVERAGE

My top competitors were my colleagues, a group of very seasoned salespeople. Whenever we closed a sale, there was a lot of paperwork that went along with the order. I was spending a lot of my time doing paperwork, and one day one of my mentors said to me, "Let me give you a piece of advice: hire an assistant. You should be spending most of your time in front of customers. You should be selling, not pushing paper." He shared an important, literally life-saving sales process principle with me that day: **the best use of a salesperson's time is either being in front of a prospect or preparing to be in front of a prospect.**

My mentor knew this. He challenged me to move beyond my comfort zone and leverage my time—to spend as much of my day as humanly possible either wrestling my way onto a prospect's calendar or taking full advantage of a time slot that I had won. He pushed me to spend most of my time doing what salespeople do best: moving relationships forward. In lots of different ways, I'm going to be challenging you to do exactly the same thing in this book. You don't have to hire your own assistant, but you do have to commit to making the most of your own time.

"Days are expensive. When you spend a day you have one less day to spend. So make sure you spend each one wisely."
~ JIM ROHN

In my case, I hired an assistant for $15 an hour. I bought her a computer and trained her to use it. These investments of time and money came out of my own calendar and my own pocket. I had a modest base salary, but I earned 10 percent commission on new business. I was giving my assistant a huge percentage of my base salary so that I could maximize my own time to earn bigger commissions.

The other salespeople who were working at the company thought I was crazy. Regardless, my assistant and I set up a daily schedule, and we started executing that schedule together. The results were very exciting. My mentor had been absolutely right: the more time I spent with prospects, the better my commission totals were. In fact, after only a couple of months, I was doing so well that the company told me I had to work from home, because the rest of the team thought I had an unfair advantage!

I really didn't think I had an unfair advantage—any one of those salespeople could have hired an assistant out of their own funds, just as I had done. But I realized something: they weren't ready to do what I had done. They were too used to the routine that the company had set up for them or that they had set up for themselves. Whichever it was, they weren't really interested in looking at another way of doing things. They weren't interested in moving beyond their comfort zones. They were more interested in working a familiar process than in working one that maximized their time and potential. That isn't the way I look at selling, and I hope it's not the way you look at selling either.

The only unfair advantage I had was this: I was willing to take responsibility for perfecting my own sales process. You can put the same unfair advantage to work on your behalf.

OWNING YOUR SALES PROCESS

When I left the office and started working from home, it felt like I was running my own little company. My day was my own, and my results were my own, too. I was winning two, three, and four deals a week—and these were pretty big deals. Because I was willing to move beyond my comfort zone, my income more than doubled. My willingness to do things a little differently meant that I was running a whole new process—*my* sales process. I was the one who was responsible for planning my day, and I was the one who was responsible for troubleshooting things at the end of the day. It wasn't the sales manager's job to manage my process: it was my job.

I liked the challenge of running a little business of my own. For it to succeed, I had to build and refine the plan that would support it. The plan eventually became a selling process, the process eventually became a whole new business (Gunpowderbusiness, which I own and run), and the business eventually led me to perfect the Gunpowder Bulletproof Prospecting System and, ultimately, to write this book. So here's the part I want you to remember: most of the strategies I developed involved doing what other salespeople were not used to doing.

Think of the salespeople in that office where I had been working. They really didn't want to have to look at a daily reminder of how someone else had created a new process—a process that might have worked for them, too, if they had been willing to try something new. Can you imagine how much it cost them financially to keep doing the same things they were used to doing, just because they were used to them? How much better off would they have been if they had adopted some of the ideas I had created? How much better off would they have been if they'd each had a mentor who was willing to push them just a little bit beyond their comfort zone? I want to be that kind of mentor for you.

Your most important weapon is your sales process. Most salespeople have a borrowed sales process, one they've inherited and never really made their own. My question for you as we get started is: "Do you own your own sales process?" The way you use your time reflects the degree of ownership you have over your sales process.

Let me repeat this point, because it is worth remembering, worth repeating to yourself each and every working day: the very best use of a salesperson's time is either being in front of a prospect or preparing to be in front of a prospect.

If you're getting distracted with something else, you're not in full ownership of your sales process. You must own your sales process completely. If you are ready to assume accountability for your own process, then you can transform your life—just as I transformed mine.

WHY WILL YOU GO THE EXTRA MILE?

Freedom has been the biggest motivator in my career. Before we go any further, I'd like to challenge you to get a little more specific about **your motivation**. What is your big WHY? You'll need it when you struggle to overcome whatever obstacles are waiting for you. What is going to drive you to think a little differently? What is going to drive you to go the extra mile?

I lived the first 40 years of my life driven by fear. I won't get into all the disastrous things I went through in my youth, but I will share with you that I wanted my daughter to have a very different childhood than the one I had. My compelling reasons for success were my daughter and my family.

I'd like you to focus on your motivation—your why—because this kind of work is tough. In my career, I've experienced some significant success as a professional salesperson. And, as the saying goes, I'm not a rocket scientist. I just worked really hard, kept learning, kept moving forward, and kept refining what I already knew. When it was challenging, I kept going because I was highly motivated to provide for my daughter, Natasha.

Where my colleagues might have met with 10 C-level contacts in a year, I would meet with 50. I pushed myself. I did things a little differently. I didn't wait for my sales manager to give me everything I needed or complain when I had to do a few things for myself. Why? Because I wanted freedom for myself and my daughter.

What do you want?

"The man who can drive himself further once the effort gets painful is the man who will win."
~ ROGER BANNISTER

Fortunately, I met a few good people along the way, and I was always eager to learn from them. A pivotal moment came when I participated in Brian Tracy's sales seminar for the very first time. I was feeling overwhelmed emotionally, and Brian's Phoenix Seminar filled the gap. He showed me how successful people become successful. I wanted to incorporate so many of the good habits he'd shared that I started working with Gregory Cleary at Peak Performance Training, Brian Tracy's sales training organization. I did that so that I could facilitate Brian's seminar!

This was the point at which I really began to turn my life around. Brian and Greg gave me a road map and started me thinking about this question: "What do successful people do differently?" It was a life-changing question.

The desire for freedom was what eventually motivated me to make major changes in my life, and I know I'm certainly not the only salesperson who's been motivated by that yearning for freedom. The other strong motivator for salespeople, in my experience, is greed. Greed really does work, no matter what people may say about it. It is certainly one of the best motivating tools I know of for turning run-of-the-mill salespeople into the trained professionals I call Gunpowderbusiness Development Managers.

In order to successfully utilize the Gunpowder Bulletproof Prospecting System, you need to consider what will motivate you. What is your BIG reason why? Is it a desire to take care of someone you love? A yearning for freedom? A desire to achieve wealth and status? Be sure to take the time to think about this carefully, because when challenges arise, and they will, you need to be clear about your motivation and your ultimate goal. That is what will keep you disciplined and focused.

GETTING THE TOOLS

Why is it necessary to stock your own toolbox? There are two reasons: sales managers are not always capable of pulling together the tools to support their sales teams and a lot of sales managers are really marketing people rather than salespeople. As a result, they have no clue what to arm their salespeople with. Very often, the tools that will make the difference are **incredibly simple,** but the salespeople don't have access to them.

These two problems often result in disaster when sales managers and small business owners hire a sales executive and think of that person as a magic bullet who will save the company and bring in all kinds of new revenue. That's a lot of pressure, and it's sometimes a symptom that something is seriously wrong within the organization. This magic bullet syndrome is particularly likely to play out in situations where the owner or founder of the business—who has been serving as the chief rainmaker—keeps hiring potential magic bullets, but can't seem to find anyone who is "good enough" to step in and fulfill the role.

That's how the entrepreneur or VP of Marketing describes the problem, but I can tell you from experience that it usually turns out that the magic bullet salesperson has never been given the strategies, information, and tools necessary to sell at the level that will ensure success.

For example, after Citytv, I went to work for a new dot-com company called DWL Inc. in Toronto. I went from working with a well-known brand like Citytv to a no-name brand. I had to figure out how to get meetings with Chief Information Officers of tier one accounts in the United States, even though I had absolutely no understanding of the technology I was selling.

I was working with enterprise technology: capturing data from old legacy systems and taking it out to consumers and making transactional websites. Everybody uses that kind of thing today, but back then computers were a relatively new thing. (Keep in mind that when I first started at Citytv, only managers had computers. The sales team did not.)

The owners of DWL didn't care that I could barely use email. They had hired me as a magic bullet—what they cared about was my history of sales success. They felt confident that they could support me with the technology side of things, and they did. They sent the president of the company to accompany me on my initial sales calls.

Now, I have to tell you that getting these meetings was not easy. I would call CIOs and work the process you'll be learning about in this book. Sometimes it would take me months to finally get a CIO to agree to meet with me. Twice, I had the CIO call me back and cancel the meeting after going to our website.

The company website, I realized, was a real problem. You see, DWL was made up of a lot of young, brilliant people. Our website reflected the youthful, creative energy of the company. It was black with lots of cool interactive elements on it. What it didn't do was resonate with the decision makers we were trying to meet with. This made my job five times harder than it had to be. (An important lesson I learned at DWL was this one: your website must resonate with the decision makers you are trying to meet with...and that means using larger font sizes and clear, can't-miss-it layouts if your decision makers are over the age of 40.)

Website problem or no website problem, I had to figure it out. Fortunately, I was able to use the Bulletproofing system I had developed at Citytv to help me, and I took us into 50 tier one accounts across the U.S. marketplace in my first year at DWL.

I had a magic bullet counterpart on the insurance side of the business who had been hired a couple of weeks after me. He was quite knowledgeable about the insurance companies who made up his target market. He had sold millions of dollars worth of technology to CIOs in the past. He was 10 times more effective in a meeting with a CIO then I was when I first started at DWL. He had a track record of proven sales success.

Unfortunately, he simply did not have the tools to overcome the big barriers that we had in getting the first meeting. He could only take us to two big opportunities in that first year, and in the end he was not with us the following year. It was tragic, because I consider him a very gifted salesperson.

The process I will be sharing with you can prevent this from happening to you. It will enable you to have complete control over your own destiny and leave nothing to chance as long as you're willing to create the sales tools you need—for yourself. It's not hard to do, but it does require that you change your routine.

As you read these words, it's possible you've entered a dry spell, and if you have, you're in luck. There is no better antidote for a slump or recession than the Gunpowder Bulletproof Prospecting System. This system is practical, relevant, useful, and proven to lead to higher market share and bigger commissions in both up and down markets, and in virtually all industries. What you'll be encountering in future chapters has turned around countless down cycles for both businesses and underperforming sales professionals.

Turning things around is my specialty. I love turning around careers, sales departments, and entire organizations when they're facing hard times. I love to watch them go from being ready to lay people off to dominating their market and growing aggressively while everyone they're competing with is still struggling.

If you know what motivates you, this system will turn things around— assuming you are willing to implement it and willing to go beyond your comfort zone. We've proven it over and over again with our clients, which is why they've responded so positively to this content. The kinds of turnarounds I'm talking about, for both individuals and organizations, allowed our clients to generate over $280 million in revenue in one recent year, using the same strategic campaign you're about to learn.

If you're willing to help yourself—to go a little bit beyond your comfort zone to turn around a down cycle in your business, your sales department, or your own career...turn the page, and I will share with you how you can begin the process of blasting open big doors.

CHAPTER TWO

Moving Beyond Fear

"Courage is fear holding on a minute longer."
~ GENERAL GEORGE S. PATTON JR.

If you are still reading, I hope it's because you are fully committed to owning your own sales process and eager to begin that process by prospecting at the highest possible level of your target organization. Your mission is a top-level prospecting mission. It requires both courage and persistence. You are going to maximize your time. You are not going to waste time calling people who aren't decision makers.

But before I explain the specific tactics in the Gunpowder Bulletproof Prospecting System, I'd like to address one of the key reasons why salespeople fail—fear. Most salespeople are afraid of calling at the top levels of the companies they are trying to sell to. As a result, most salespeople are not persistent in their prospecting. Most salespeople are afraid to try something different. Remember, if you continue to do what most salespeople do, you'll continue to get the results that most salespeople get. Our mission demands that we try something different. To do that, we must embrace fear: fear of the unfamiliar, fear of rejection, fear of failure, fear of looking foolish.

It's okay to feel scared at first—if you are committed, you will move forward anyway. It's human nature to feel fear whenever you step out of your comfort zone. I have found that the very best way to conquer fear is to do the things you fear.

"Do the thing you fear and the death of fear is certain."
~ RALPH WALDO EMERSON

Our mission demands that we go into the marketplace to locate allies who can help us get to the high-level people we must reach out to. Our mission: wrestle our way onto the radar screens of these allies and to stay in front of them until we identify the people with signing authority and budget, the people who can make a decision. Our mission demands persistence! The reasons we target the top are simple: to accelerate the sales cycle and to keep ourselves from chasing dead ends. Let's face it: people who are afraid to call at the top spend weeks getting referred to people with no authority, and they end up failing.

Top-level prospecting means:

- Make the call. Feel the fear and doing it anyway, no matter how uncomfortable you feel.
- Persevere. Never give up. Keep calling.
- Be professional at all times. Remember, we are in the service business.
- Make it worth their while. Have real value to share with people. Remember, we help people.

I've learned the importance of these four elements from direct experience countless times. You will learn their importance as you implement the principles I'll be sharing with you.

WHO GAVE YOU THIS NUMBER?

Years ago, I was looking for an appointment with a senior vice president at Imperial Oil, one who was in charge of all telecom spending. I had tried dozens of times to get to the president's office, but after all that effort, I was still getting nowhere. Nobody I talked to at Imperial Oil would give out a name. Now, I always try to get the help of the CEO's executive assistant. In my 15-plus years of selling to Fortune 1000 companies, I've learned that the EA usually knows who is in charge. In this case, though, I couldn't even get the name of the executive assistant to the president. But

I kept trying. Why? Because good prospecting means not giving up. I was always pleasant. I was always professional. I was always willing to bring a positive attitude to each and every person I talked to at Imperial Oil. And I was not giving up!

One day, I was reaching out to Imperial Oil again, and I struck up a conversation with a receptionist I had never talked to before. By this point, I was quite familiar with all the voices of the receptionists who were answering the phone at Imperial Oil. This new receptionist and I had very good chemistry right off the bat, and after a few moments of chatting, I asked her for the name of the executive assistant in the president's office. She gave it to me, and I called the president's assistant. The first question she asked was, "How did you get this number?" How would you have answered that?

That was a scary moment, but I didn't give up my source. I simply said that my manager had told me to get in touch with the president of Imperial Oil. After all, I had built up a relationship with an ally, and I wasn't about to betray her. What I did do, though, was have the first of a series of good conversations with one of the president's five executive assistants. As a result, I ended up winning another ally. As you will learn, building up rapport with executive assistants and turning them into allies is an important part of the Gunpowder Bulletproof Prospecting System.

I eventually received a referral from the president's office for a meeting with the senior vice president in charge of purchasing in my area. What would have happened if I had stopped calling Imperial Oil after the third or fourth call that went nowhere? What would have happened if I had stopped calling after a dozen calls? What would have happened if I had stopped looking for new allies I could connect with at Imperial Oil? Perseverance makes all the difference.

One thing I know about companies like Imperial Oil—companies that have gatekeeping down to an impenetrable art—is that once you get in, you have effectively differentiated yourself. The barriers are so strongly fortified that very few people actually get past the gatekeeper. That means the people you end up talking to are usually a lot nicer to you than those at companies that allow salespeople relatively easy access to their top executives. Remember: tens of thousands of good salespeople are prospecting the best companies in the world. Top executives are tired of being prospected. In order to stand out, you need to come to the phone with *no fear*, **with real value**, and with the energy of unyielding service. Forget about selling. Nobody likes to be sold to. Just keep moving forward with an attitude of service.

Prospecting is a mission, and the first rule of that mission is not to give up. You have to make a commitment to never stop looking for allies.

Sure, people are sometimes stern, brusque, or even rude while you're still on the outside trying to get in. That's when most salespeople feel the fear—and give up. This is when you'll need to focus on your motivation on your "Big Why " to help keep you moving forward. If you keep looking for openings, keep looking for new allies, keep making the effort to connect, you will find that when you finally do get in there are people who will indeed benefit from your product or service, and they are waiting for you.

MAKE FEAR WORK FOR YOU

I have seen many people quit because they became immobilized by fear. They would let fear stop them from picking up the phone and reaching out to their ideal prospect. You must take the opposite approach. You must make fear your friend, and use its energy to drive you forward.

In this book, I will be asking you to do a lot of things that will not be second nature to you. You may feel like backing away from these things. It's actually good that you initially feel scared about the things I'll be putting on your to-do list...as long as you can harness that fear and make it work for you. It is not enough to read this book—you have to execute and persevere without letting yourself be overcome by fear.

When I began working with Gregory Cleary, my sales manager at Peak Performance Training, I was scared out of my mind every morning. My biggest fear was rejection. To help me overcome the fear of picking up the phone, I would start every day by calling a girlfriend. In no time, we would be laughing and joking about life, and that energy stayed with me. Do you see what I did? My first few calls right after speaking with my best friend were driven not so much by the fear, but by my response to the fear—namely, the decision to call my girlfriend. That's how I channeled the energy. Thanks to her call, I could keep the same energy and optimism as I began my work.

Before long, I was able to pretend that everyone I was calling was my best friend. My tonality was so inviting that people warmed up to me quickly and my fear dissipated. I kept going until I hit my goal of booking three new meetings for the day. You, too, need a response to fear.

---

*"A hero is no braver than an ordinary man,
but he is brave five minutes longer."*
~ RALPH WALDO EMERSON

I was also scared out of my mind when I worked at Citytv. I had a million-dollar quota, only a few small accounts to start with, no useable marketing materials, a whole lot of debt from my failed marriage, and I was a single mother. I had to come up with some serious support mechanisms to keep me going. Here were my responses to the fear I felt:

- I made my to-do list the night before, so that in the morning, when I was at my best, I could make the most of my first round of calls.
- I worked out in the morning, before I left for work.
- I called my best friend on my drive to work.
- I listened to great music or motivational tapes after talking to my friend.
- I focused my time on what I call "high payoff activities." These were my answers to the question, "What is going to bring in new clients?" I ask myself that question all the time.
- I did things to keep my energy up and avoided doing things that brought my energy down (like drinking alcohol).

ONE LESS THING TO FEAR

Another big thing I did to get past fear early on in my career was to execute on a major life decision: I resolved to carry no financial debt. When I worked at London Life Insurance Company, I was shown a national statistic—less then 5 percent of people retire without needing assistance of some kind. Less than 5 percent! I made a decision right then and there that I was going to be in that 5 percent. I was going to save my money.

I had plenty of colleagues who were maxed out on their credit cards. They didn't do too well because they were constantly stressed and fearful about money. You don't need that kind of extra stress when you're pushing yourself into situations that are outside of your comfort zone.

Different people have different stress points. Fear of not having enough money is a big one for most people, and it certainly was for me. I decided that the only way for me to win this fight with fear was to have six months of savings put away. Yes, this means I lived well under my means for a while.

If you are serious about moving beyond fear, and I hope you are, my advice is that you become a great saver. It's simply amazing how **money attracts money**. Years ago, one of the people in my Mastermind peer group shared a life-changing principle: pay yourself first. This means that you decide in advance how much money you can save every week (10 percent is a good place to start) and you put that money in a long-term account. This is money you never spend. It's money you invest wisely and conservatively. Now, keep in mind that at the time I was working hard to pay down my big debt from my failed marriage. When I first heard this principle I thought, "No, I have to put every dime toward my debt." Let me tell you that saving money is a muscle you have to start training, and thank God I listened to my mentors. Start today no matter what your situation is!

As soon as I started this pay-yourself-first system, the law of attraction kicked in. I started to feel different: doors started to open a little more easily, my commissions started to come a little faster, people started referring me to more opportunities. The results were amazing. Fear was less of an influence, and I started attracting bigger and bigger deals. My paychecks literally doubled the year I started this habit, and I now make a point of recommending to all my clients that they keep their debt low. I believe money attracts money, while debt attracts fear. Which do you want in your life?

"A man in debt is so far a slave."
~ RALPH WALDO EMERSON

GROWING OR ROTTING?

The fact is many people never manage to break through the fear. They interpret fear as a signal to retreat instead of looking at it as humanity's great motivator. One of my favorite human potential trainers, Jim Quinn, used to say, "People are a lot like fruit. When you're green, you grow. When you're ripe, you rot." Who wants to rot?

Yes, fear is a natural human response to risk, but people who refuse to take any risks inevitably begin to rot. They tend to live their whole lives with a feeling of dread. Don't be one of those people! Try to conquer a fear every year. By doing this, you will make fear your best friend.

"Pushing through fear is less frightening than living with the underlying fear that comes from feelings of helplessness."
~ SUSAN JEFFERS

MY FRIEND FEAR

Fear was my friend for 40 years. I can see that now, looking back. Fear gave me the energy to get up at 5:00 AM, work out, and be in the office and on the phone by 7:00 AM. I invite you to change your view of fear. Change your psychology around fear. Begin to see fear as your friend, the friend that gives you the adrenalin to break through obstacles. Fear is nature's energy source; it actually comes to help you, to motivate you, and to give you the energy to blast through any obstacle that comes your way.

Whenever you step outside your comfort zone, it's natural that feelings of fear will come along. If you can learn to embrace them instead of shying away, what new possibilities will open up for you?

A great way to conquer fear is to adopt a high level of self-discipline. Did you know that every time you exercise self-discipline your self-esteem goes up? Whenever you delay doing something fun and easy for something hard and necessary your self-esteem goes up. Every act of self-discipline increases your personal power. You like yourself better, and you increase your self-respect. Raise your self-esteem every day by exercising self-discipline. Greater self-esteem will help you to face your fear and move forward through it.

Think of courage as a muscle you can train. The more you practice, the easier it gets. When you first rode a bicycle did you do so without any training wheels? No, you used some support until your confidence was strong. Well, it's the same thing with Gunpowder's Bulletproof Prospecting System—we put supports around you so that you feel confident enough to move beyond the fear and begin blasting open big doors.

Chapter THREE

Bulletproofing Yourself

*"Success demands a high level of logistical
and organizational competence."*

~ General George S. Patton Jr.

The Gunpowder Bulletproof Prospecting System is all about accelerating your success. However, before I get into the specifics of the program, I'd like to discuss Bulletproofing and why it is so important to your success. What is Bulletproofing? Bulletproofing yourself means protecting yourself from rejection and protecting yourself from looking foolish. It means learning how to influence people to your way of thinking, preparing for the "no" with smart questions, and preparing for the 10 most common objections to taking a meeting. All of this is grounded in understanding the real benefits your product or service has to offer. By doing the necessary preparation correctly, competently, and thoroughly you will exude a confidence that will generate a tremendous amount of respect.

Some salespeople go into the marketplace without doing any preparation or market research. That's not only a failure for them, it's also a failure for the management team that is letting them go out unprepared. I recently met with a sales manager and his new hire, a magic bullet he had poached from a competitor. When I asked them the three big reasons people do business with them, they floundered for about an hour. You don't get an hour to prove your worth in a top-level meeting. They were unclear about the real value that differentiated them from their main competitor. They had never bothered to ask their customers. This is one of the top three companies in their field. Let me ask you—is this the kind of sales manager you want to be working with?

If you don't know the answer to the basic questions "What's your value?" and "How do you stack up against the competition and win?" then you're reading the right book. The Gunpowder Bulletproof Prospecting System shows you the step-by-step way to Bullet proof yourself and your team.

Salespeople who are not properly Bullet proofed are easy to recognize. They might:

- Fail to get appointments with the right people.
- Fail to sell their product. (They're more likely to be "order-takers" than salespeople who are Bullet proofed.)
- Get a hot lead and then try to "power close" it.
- Essentially treat each prospect as identical to every other prospect.
- Ask few questions (or no questions) of their prospects.
- Don't know what questions the most successful salespeople in their organization ask.
- Don't know how to address the most common objections.
- Have no sense of their company's mission in the marketplace.
- Have no sense of their personal mission for their customers.
- Spend an inordinate amount of time blathering on in small talk mode.
- Go into long lectures about their product or service. (We call this the Shiny Red Ball Syndrome, which is something you'll learn about in a minute.)

Because any one of these problems is enough to make a target prospect glaze over and disengage, you will not begin any part of your prospecting process without first doing proper Bulletproofing.

Bulletproofing means being prepared and that is why it is the centre of the Gunpowder Bulletproof Prospecting System. Bulletproofing means knowing enough about the company you're calling on, and enough about the value you can add to that company, to sound confident about it during a discussion. It means understanding what the target organization's pain points are before you pick up the phone. It means understanding exactly what people are struggling with now; so that you can speak confidently and sincerely about how you can help them do things better.

"Leaders think and talk about the solutions. Followers think and talk about the problems."

~ Brian Tracy

The Shiny Red Ball

First and foremost, you must accept personal responsibility for doing all of your homework *before* you pick up the phone, so you don't have to fall back on the deadly habit of talking about your product's feature set. This is (let's face it) boring to the people you are targeting. And being boring is an unforgiveable sin when you are prospecting. The keys to Bulletproofing are to uncover the value you offer your clients and to understand how you stack up against the competition.

One of the biggest mistakes salespeople make is falling prey to the "Shiny Red Ball Syndrome." Imagine these people are selling a big red ball. What do they want to talk about? The ball, of course: "Look how nice our ball is. Look how high it bounces when I drop it to the floor. Listen to the sound it makes as it bounces. Notice how vibrant this particular shade of red is. Isn't our ball the best? So, would you like to buy my shiny red ball?" This is typically a sign of nervousness; nervousness that's rooted, whether the salesperson knows it or not, in a lack of proper Bulletproofing. Sales discussions about the shiny red ball inevitably result in failure.

The first step to Bulletproofing is to accept that you *must* avoid talking about yourself and your product until you understand your customer's needs and priorities—why did they agree to see you? No ball is red enough, shiny enough, or bounces high enough to lead the discussion. You can avoid this pitfall by doing the necessary research to understand your value proposition and your client's needs *before* you pick up the phone. In Chapter 5 I'll take you through a step-by-step process to accomplish this.

WHY SALESPEOPLE FAIL TO BULLETPROOF THEMSELVES

Failure to Bulletproof often comes about when we have an unrealistic view of what our job as salespeople really is. For instance, our job is not to be the most dominant person in the room.

Not long ago, the president of a big marketing firm I was working with brought me in for an initial meeting with a huge international organization he wanted to work with. He started rattling on and on about his company and all its accomplishments. As I looked around the room, I could see the expressions on the faces of the three top-level people he'd brought in for the meeting, and all three of them were glazing over.

The president of this marketing company kept yammering on about his company and how fantastic it was. He did not seem to realize that these important players were tuning out of the meeting. At one point there was a brief pause, (I almost think my client must have stopped, for the first time, to take a breath) and I jumped in with a question for our prospects: "What are you hoping to learn today?"

The three contacts perked up and started talking. I started taking notes and encouraging them to talk more. That's what salespeople do—get decision makers to talk! That's what our first and most important job is, throughout the sales process. If our prospects aren't talking, we are guilty of malpractice.

In essence, I had saved the meeting. But afterwards, my client pulled me aside and said, "Christine, there can only be one leader in the meeting!" I guess he expected me to sit on my hands when I could tell that people were tuning out. He never won that business, because it was more important to him to be the "top dog" in the room than it was to ask questions that would allow us to figure out how we could help.

That is the key question: "How do we help the client?" After all, salespeople are in the business of service. Unfortunately, the president didn't realize that he wasn't helping anyone by talking at length about his own company. If being top dog during the prospecting call, or at any phase of the sale, is more important to you than anything else, then being top dog is too expensive. Leave your shiny red ball at home.

MENTAL BULLETPROOFING: WORKING FROM ABUNDANCE

We'll elaborate on the steps for logistically Bullet proofing yourself in the next few chapters. But before you're ready to pick up the phone and start setting meetings, you must also be mentally Bullet proofed. Your calls must be connected to a goal, and not just any goal. They must be connected to the right personal goal for the day, the week, and the month. If they're not, then you're still not Bullet proofed mentally. Here's a true story that may help to explain what I mean:

Diana, a new hire at my company, was very excited after having completed her initial training with us. She came into my office and said, "Christine, I want you to know that I've just started work on my first account. I'm going to book 10 meetings this week!"

I appreciated her enthusiasm and I told her as much. Even so, I was a little concerned that her goal was too aggressive. Ten new quality meetings with real decision makers at Fortune 1000 companies in the first week is unheard of from one of our new people. So, while I made sure to tell Diana that I liked her can-do attitude, I also let her know that I would very be happy if she booked one qualified meeting that week.

You can probably tell already that Diana was one of those profoundly goal-driven people, and that is certainly a wonderful trait. She was also someone who believed in sharing her goals out loud with other people, which is also wonderful. In her case, though, I was wondering what not hitting her stated goal of scheduling 10 meetings during the first week would do to her attitude.

The next week, I found out. It turned out that my concerns about the goal being too ambitious were well justified. Diana had failed to set a single meeting in her first week of calling, and as the week went along, she dug herself into a deeper and deeper pit of disappointment. It became clear to me that Diana's first week of calling had not motivated her, but had crushed her. Whereas last week I had been talking to an upbeat, enthusiastic, and positive team player, I was now dealing with someone who was clearly humiliated, and who was trying not to meet my gaze in the hallway. Unfortunately, she didn't bounce back from that experience.

What happened? Diana had set herself up for failure. She had set an unrealistic early goal for herself, and the emotional ramifications of not hitting that goal had made it impossible for her to *work from abundance*.

Diana would have been much better off if she'd set a more realistic daily goal for herself, attained it, and expanded from there. If she'd done that, she would have been working from abundance. It would have been much easier for her to achieve her goal and raise her self-esteem.

Let me be very clear on this one point: the system I am laying out for you in this book simply will not work for you if you don't understand and support the simple idea of working from abundance.

Working from abundance means:

- Hitting modest targets first and ramping upwards once you attain them.

- Drawing on your own reservoirs of confidence and optimism.

- Knowing that you always have enough new leads to call and enough new opportunities to pursue.

- Understanding that you can always bounce back no matter what happens.

- Feeling certain that you are on your game whenever you pick up the phone.

- Being secure enough in yourself and your own abilities to say, "Next!" whenever people give you a hard time on the phone. (You should actually be ecstatic when that happens, because you've just gotten clear confirmation that you were calling too low in the organization and should be talking to someone else. I'll share more on this point in a later chapter.)

Working from abundance perpetuates itself over time. Happy people attract positive responses, and positive responses make a positive outlook easier. A positive outlook when you are calling means that abundance follows you on your calls.

Unfortunately, Diana was only working from abundance for roughly one half of her very first full day of calling for us. She had a great attitude for the first couple of hours, but by the time lunch rolled around, she realized she hadn't scheduled any meetings. After that, she was working from desperation, and working from desperation doesn't work.

Have you ever been demotivated by unrealistic goals? If so, you've been denying yourself the opportunity to work from abundance.

Take a Closer Look

As part of your own preparation for the mental combat that is selling, I want to challenge you to look more closely, right now, at what happened to Diana, and then consider how her experience relates to your world. Once again, here's what happened:

She got off to a bad start (in her own mind). She then started thinking about how terrible it was going to feel when she had to admit to me (and everyone else she had told about her aggressive goal) that she wasn't going to hit her target. Her day, and her critical first week, began to get worse and worse.

How much better off would she have been if she had given herself this goal for her first day: "Find the name and contact information for *one* decision maker at twenty of the companies on my lead list." (By the way, that is now the first calling goal we give to everybody who starts with us.) My bet is that Diana would have hit that goal well before lunchtime on her first day, and would have been working from abundance all day long as a result.

She could have easily ramped up to a new, slightly more aggressive goal, secure in the knowledge that she was on her game. Her whole outlook on her job, and on herself, would have been very different.

Set the Right Calling Goal

Once you do start calling, your goal for the first day of calling is going to be the goal I should have made sure Diana bought into. Here it is again:

Find the name and contact information for *one* decision maker at twenty of the companies on your lead list. This includes email addresses for the decision maker and/or the decision maker's executive assistant.

This is a great initial goal, especially if you don't like to pick up the phone. The act of navigating the gatekeepers is a great way to warm up. In no time you will see for yourself that people really can be friendly and helpful, and it's a great way to refine your target acquisition list, which we'll discuss in more detail later.

You can expand your goals from there, and you can also have a great time doing it.

MENTAL BULLETPROOFING IN ACTION

Recently I was at a party where there were a lot of unmarried women who were obviously "on the prowl" for a man with whom they could start a relationship. Now, you should know that I'm happily married, I wear a pretty obvious wedding ring, my husband was with me at this party, and I wasn't dressing (or acting) in any particularly flirtatious way. In short, it was obvious that I wasn't "in the market." Yet, for some strange reason, I was attracting conversations with just about every man in the room, and drawing glares from all the single women at that party. Every available guy, it seemed, was eager to get my attention.

Why? It wasn't my attire, my hairstyle, or any other external thing. It was the fact that I make a habit of working and living from abundance. That had carried over to the party my husband and I had chosen to go to that Sunday afternoon. I was smiling, I was talking optimistically, I wasn't taking myself too seriously, I was actually enjoying myself. As a result, I was attractive to other people at that party.

People really are attracted to optimism. They are attracted to people who enjoy themselves. They are really not attracted to desperation. I hate to have to say it, but that's how those single women at the party were coming across—as desperate, as driven, as running out of time. Do you like to spend time with people like that? Or talk to them? Me neither.

Take a lesson from my experience at that party. You now know how to make a *bad* impression. Use that knowledge and make sure the impression you leave is a good one. Whenever you're on the phone, you must *be*—not just act, but actually be—positive, upbeat, and engaging. You have to sound like you're inviting someone to have a great time with you at a party, not like you're inviting someone to a morgue.

FINAL THOUGHTS ON ABUNDANCE

Everyone who sells for me takes this responsibility of working and living from abundance very seriously. They develop specific strategies for getting themselves into a positive, upbeat, approachable frame of mind *before* they pick up the phone. These strategies include:

- Going to the gym or for a brisk walk for an hour a day.
- Listening to upbeat music or motivational training tapes.
- Listening to comedy.
- Yoga
- Calling a friend or family member who always makes them feel great.
- Changing their physical posture when they make calls.
- Meditating. (I highly recommend Deepak Chopra's guidance on this subject. You can learn more about the Chopra Center at www. chopra.com, where they have many free meditations available online)
- Getting together with friends on a regular basis.
- Seeing inspiring film or plays.
- Shopping!

- Improv acting classes
- Going to the gym (it's worth repeating)

You must be genuinely happy before you pick up the phone to call anyone on your lead list. Not fake happy, genuinely happy. That's Bulletproofing yourself for mental combat: getting yourself into that state of mind before each and every call.

Exercising and eating well are long-term lifestyle changes that will support you in your efforts to spend more and more of your time working and living from abundance. These lifestyle improvements are critically important, because you do need energy and enthusiasm to be a good salesperson.

"A salesman, like the storage battery in your car, is constantly discharging energy. Unless he is recharged frequently he soon runs dry."
~ ZIG ZIGLAR

I believe sales is ultimately an exchange of enthusiasm, and I also believe that one of the fastest ways to accelerate any sale is to increase the energy level in the relationship in a positive way. To do that, you need to be in great shape, not just mentally, but physically.

If you are serious about working and living from abundance, and I hope you are, you will commit to a daily workout routine of some kind, and work, each day, toward becoming what I call a lean, smart, fighting machine. Not a lean, mean, fighting machine, (because nobody likes a bully) but a lean, smart, fighting machine—someone who is persistent about uncovering the hidden reasons why someone who really needs what you have to offer does not see the value you bring (yet!) with your product or service.

Do This Now

Before you move on to the next chapter, please come up with at least three specific activities that will get you into a happy, upbeat, positive, and optimistic state of mind. Once you have these three activities clear in your mind, you must practice them to make sure that they really do put you in an attractive frame of mind for the party that is your next call.

Most salespeople, of course, are allowed (and even encouraged!) to go into battle completely unprepared—to march into an ambush that doesn't have to happen. I think one of the big reasons salespeople are so willing to jump into the field of battle without sufficiently Bulletproofing themselves is the nagging feeling that they have to do something. After all, the sales manager is watching!

What should you really be doing? Preparing for battle. By taking the time to Bulletproof yourself by preparing both logistically and mentally, you'll be better equipped to handle any obstacles in your way.

CHAPTER FOUR

Your Tactical Plan: The 4 Elements of Top Level Prospecting

"Accept the challenges so you can feel the exhilaration of victory."
~ GENERAL GEORGE S. PATTON JR.

The guaranteed way to double your business is to become an expert at prospecting. Remember, your mission is top-level prospecting, and you must carry out this mission according to a clear, specific plan. Now that you've learned about the importance of Bulletproofing yourself, it's time to talk strategy. You need a tactical plan—the Gunpowder Bulletproof Prospecting System is that plan. It's a 4-point tactical plan. Each tactic supports the next, and each one gets you closer to your mission objective—booking meeting after meeting after meeting. This prospecting methodology has been battle tested in the marketplace and will work in any industry across the globe, including yours, to create openings and alliances with senior decision makers—if you work the plan. The Gunpowder Bulletproof Prospecting System is everything you need for success!

Let's look at the four parts of the plan, and pay close attention, because this is your mission overview:

Your Tactical Plan

TACTIC ONE: BASIC TRAINING AND RECONNAISSANCE

This is the critical intelligence gathering stage of your mission, where you learn everything you need to know *before* reaching out to a given market. The information you gather will help you to develop clear benefit statements that will resonate with the people you're trying to reach. Notice that I said "statements"—you will arm yourself not just with one benefit statement, but with many. Before you do anything else, you must research the world in which your target decision maker operates and identify a minimum of three great reasons for someone to put you on their calendar.

Mike Netter (one of my clients) calls this the Power of Three, but some of my salespeople at the Gunpowder offices put together as many as **10 benefit statements** before picking up the phone and calling people. Personally, I'd rather be supported by the Power of Ten: 10 good reasons why your product or service is beneficial to a prospect. Regardless of the number you choose for your first task, **you must learn to articulate these benefits concisely** and from multiple angles before you reach out to your target organization.

Following our weekly sales meetings at Gunpowderbusiness, we drill all of our people on the benefit statements they'll be using in their calls that day. We make people practice delivering their benefit statements in front of the group because we know it feels a little awkward. When you deliver your benefit statements in public, you're putting yourself out in the open, and your peers can notice all the mistakes you're making. That's the point: you have to get past the initial awkwardness, which is going to be an even stronger obstacle on the phone, and you have to become hardwired to steer the conversation back to the reasons why you are absolutely certain it makes sense for this person to talk to you.

Your other key task during the Basic Training and Reconnaissance phase is to identify who you want to call in your prospective account. Your initial goals are: to find the name of the president of the organization you're reaching out to and, with this ammunition, to identify his or her executive assistant. Your ultimate goal may be simply to have someone from the president's or owner's office provide you with an internal referral to the right decision maker. If you don't know who the decision maker is, you want someone the decision maker answers to tell them to take your call. Make no mistake: the president's executive assistant is, from your perspective, the most important person in the organization. If you don't know who the executive assistant to the president or owner is, you are not ready to move onto the next tactic.

> Plan Tactic #1: Before you pick up the phone or do anything else, you must know who you will be calling, why you are calling that person, and the reasons why the meeting you want to set up makes sense from the target contact's point of view. What's in it for them?

TACTIC TWO: FIRST CONTACT

During this stage, you will make the initial contact with your target—via the perfect voice mail message. Leaving a great voice mail message for a busy decision maker gives your prospect a chance to absorb the good reasons for your call. That's important, because **the phone is interruptive.** When someone answers the phone, he or she is probably in the middle of reading email, responding to email, getting ready for a meeting, or doing any number of other things. As a result, your cold call may be viewed as an annoyance.

This begs the question: Why cold call when you can **turn every prospecting call into a warm call** by leaving great voice mail? This method ensures that your prospect has a chance to evaluate your request and get to know you ahead of time.

When we train someone new at Gunpowderbusiness, we make sure that person never speaks to a live prospect right away. It's too hard for a brand new salesperson to be rejected voice to voice. We want the new person to gain confidence by learning about our client's value proposition. So we help our people develop great voice mail messages, and we make them start with those. In fact, we don't let them go live until I have approved their voice mail message. Fear of rejection is the number one thing that holds people back from blasting open big doors. There is no rejection with voice mail!

Voice mail is an essential sales tool that far too many people ignore or misuse. Sometimes people leave a single voice mail message, don't get a call back, and assume that their work is finished. Your goal is to leave a series of entertaining, captivating, friendly voice mail messages over time. This approach can work wonders, even if you have to leave messages over a period of weeks or months. Following this part of the process gets you the most amazing responses from the person when you finally connect voice to voice. Your prospect will say things like, "I feel like I know you already!" The right voice mail message sets the stage for the whole relationship.

While more information on crafting a great voice message can be found in Chapters 7 and 8, the key is that you must not sound like you're reading from a script when you leave your message. Your initial contact with a prospect must be engaging, informative, and positive.

Remember: if you end up speaking with someone on your first contact, you're not following the process. The voice mail process is important because it creates a relationship in advance of your first voice-to-voice conversation with your prospect. Voice mail also creates a sense of familiarity with your value propositions. Well-delivered voice mail messages make your prospect a more educated consumer, one who's more familiar with your company and, usually, more receptive to you. **Voicemails turn a cold call into a warm call,** so if you find yourself on a cold call (speaking with a decision maker on your first contact), you aren't following your tactical plan.

The only exception to this is contact with executive assistants, whom you can reach out to, voice to voice, at any time. You are going to speak to several executive assistants in your hunt for the REAL decision maker. Assistants are more available and are more used to having their days interrupted. If you can make a connection with a decision maker's executive assistant, that can be a significant bonus. Executive assistants who warm to you can sometimes accelerate the prospecting process for you in ways that will pleasantly surprise you. Let them do so when the opportunity arises, but don't imagine you can work this process without leaving good initial voice mail messages, and remember to treat every executive assistant like the client—make them feel important. They are often over worked, underpaid, and underappreciated. When they meet someone who genuinely appreciates their help, wonderful things can happen.

> Plan Tactic #2: Your first contact with the decision maker will be via the perfect voice mail message. You should be prepared to leave multiple entertaining voice mail messages over time.

TACTIC THREE: ELECTRONIC WARFARE

Email is a very powerful prospecting tool, yet it never ceases to amaze me how often salespeople skip it entirely. Email allows you to connect on a one-on-one basis—to get on people's radar screens without actually being in their faces. People can examine your message at their leisure and digest your request for a meeting. Once they do that, they'll be more receptive to your call and to the idea of meeting with you.

Often decision makers want to invite a few of their colleagues to check you out as well. Arming your prospect with a great email makes it easy to invite other people to the meeting, which will accelerate your sales cycle and ensure that the right people are in the room for your meeting.

Typically, the perfect email message will be your second point of contact with your target. As you will learn in Chapter 9, there are many formats for an effective email communication, but one of the core principles is that every paragraph should be full of information about how you plan to add value. This should be backed up by client quotes concisely describing the good work you have done for others. Some people believe that long email messages never get read, but I disagree. It's the quality of the email message that determines whether or not it gets read, not the length. Remember—you are reaching out to senior executives and decision makers who did not reach these positions by skipping details. They tend to be slow and deliberate when it matters, and they are more than willing to invest their time in reading your message if they see value in that message.

If you follow the advice that I'll be sharing with you about how to craft the right email message for the selling situation you face, you'll find that email is a truly invaluable tool for establishing one-on-one contact with your prospects.

Plan Tactic #3: Follow up the perfect voice mail message with the perfect email message. Everything you write in that message should highlight the value you plan to add to your prospects and should be backed up by client quotes about your good work.

TACTIC FOUR: VOICE-TO-VOICE COMBAT

Now that you've done your homework and taken the time to warm up your prospect with the perfect voice message and an informative email, it's time to close the deal. Well, the first deal, at any rate—by getting the prospect on the phone and wrestling your way onto the right person's calendar.

Lots of salespeople tell me they don't like cold calls. I don't like them either; that's why I don't make them! If you do tactics one, two, and three correctly, you will find that this is nothing like a cold call. It's a GOLD call, because you've already given your target valuable, high-impact information that has won awareness and respect—before you even pick up the phone. This is what opens doors. Just follow through on the good work you've already done and use that experience to present key people with new ideas and new ways of looking at their business.

As with voice mail, the key here is to be proactive. Don't expect your prospect to reach out to you; less than 5 percent of prospects will call you back. It is your job, your responsibility, to continue to follow up with them to make voice-to-voice combat happen. Decision makers have a tremendous amount of stress and numerous demands for their time. They simply don't have time to call you back.

Be persistent, respectful, focused, educational, and positive. Get people live on the phone and book the meeting!

Sometimes you can even turn a brush-off into an appointment—if you keep working your plan. One of our salespeople at Gunpowderbusiness recently had a rushed, curt, seemingly unproductive call with a target decision maker he'd been tracking for weeks. He politely concluded the call and immediately sent the decision maker a value-rich email apologizing for interrupting his busy day. The very next time he called, the target booked a meeting on the spot. That's not necessarily going to happen every time, of course, but why not make life easier for yourself by making life easier for your target? Maintain a respectful, positive attitude, and make it as easy as possible for him or her to book a meeting with you.

Most salespeople skip the first three tactics of the plan and go straight to the voice-to-voice combat phase. This significantly reduces their odds, and it shows—they routinely get slaughtered. If you do the up-front work that helps your prospect become more educated and receptive to your message and to your request for his or her time, you will be more likely to get your meeting. You have to make your plan and work the process relentlessly. As I mentioned in the earlier chapters, ingraining persistence and perseverance into your work ethic will pay dividends here as you continue to work your plan, for weeks or months on end if necessary, in an upbeat, positive way.

> Plan Tactic #4: Work your plan! Get people live on the phone and book the meeting. Stay persistent. Stay focused. Stay positive.

KNOW YOUR TACTICAL PLAN

In Chapter 12, I share a possible variation on this four-tactic methodology. For now, though, what I've shared with you here is your plan. I'd like you to assume that the steps you've just read—researching, leaving a voice mail message, sending an email message, and establishing voice-to-voice contact—reflect the sequence of events you will use to set up the first scheduled meeting with a decision maker.

My four-point tactical plan has been proven effective over and over again in the global marketplace. On tough assignments, our conversion rate in a one-year period is 43 to 47 percent, and over a longer period of time that conversion rates jumps into the 90's because we never burn a bridge and we are always developing relationships with decision makers. We respect their time and their budgeting time frames. As a result, we have opened up more than 19,000 big doors for our clients over the last eight years and the plan can work for you, too. The Gunpowder Bulletproof Prospecting System is your blueprint for success, your way to open up big doors and accelerate your career. Following the plan will help you to carry out your mission. If you stick with it, you'll succeed in your mission, because you'll always know where you are and where you want to go next.

CHAPTER FIVE

Tactic 1: The Intelligence Briefing

*"Now, an army is a team. It lives, eats, sleeps,
fights as a team."*

~ General George S. Patton Jr.

This step is about arming yourself with good information so you can accelerate the sales process. When this is done correctly, your confidence can't help but double and triple as you gain a deeper understanding of the value you have to offer and how to communicate this value in a clear, concise way that captures people's interest and respect.

Your first basic training and reconnaissance assignment is to track down the highest-ranking and most successful salesperson in your organization and find a way to transfer as much of that person's knowledge as possible into your head in the shortest time span possible. This is the first part of your intelligence briefing.

If you are just starting out, you have an advantage because more experienced salespeople will be willing to mentor you. If you have been in the game for a while, you can still learn what you need by adopting great mentors. Choose people who have achieved the kind of success you admire.

Early in my sales career, I was blessed to work with senior salespeople who were willing to extend a helping hand and compress my learning curve. They were gracious enough to allow me to accompany them on sales calls. I think they recognized that most good salespeople start out from a place where they know that they have a lot to learn. I recommend that you try this and that you follow a few basic guidelines as you do so.

First and foremost, the salesperson you're going out with must be willing to introduce you and explain why you're there. The prospect should not be wondering who is playing what role or why some people are talking and others aren't. Your mentor can simply say something like, "This is my colleague Rose; she's shadowing me here today, and she's here to learn."

Of course, you must be willing to sit quietly, listen, and take notes. Remember, you're there to learn, not to be top dog. If you find you have questions about why the salesperson you're going out with did something or other, you must be willing to wait until you're out of the meeting and somewhere private to ask your question.

This kind of meeting can be a win-win situation all around: you find out essential information about best practices, the salesperson you've reached out to gets acknowledgement of his or her expertise (and the benefit of your notes), and the prospect or client gets confirmation that an experienced person is in charge of the account.

Even if it's not possible for you to arrange such a meeting, you can still offer to take the top performer you've chosen out for breakfast, lunch, or coffee so that you can get the benefit of his or her experience for an hour or so. The questions you'll ask during that meeting are going to be the same questions you'd ask on the car ride to or from the meeting with the live prospect. Regardless of the setting, you want to get this person's insights on the following:

7 CRITICAL QUESTIONS FOR YOUR MENTOR

- The three most common objections which are likely to arise when you're trying to set an appointment over the phone.
- The three best responses or turnarounds to those objections.
- The three questions most likely to determine whether or not there's really a business opportunity to pursue.
- The three most common "pain points" for a client within a specific market segment. (These, of course, are problems that your product or service can alleviate.)
- The most common titles of decision makers within a specific market segment that your company has been able to help (i.e. people who can sign the contract).
- Who the major competitors are within a specific market segment,

and how your organization stacks up against them. Ask: "When they are the incumbent, what's the best strategy for replacing them in the short term? In the long term?"

- The three best success stories your organization has delivered within a specific market segment.

That's a lot to learn, but you must learn it. It's essential to Bulletproofing yourself. Many small and medium sized businesses struggle when it comes to working all of this material into a salesperson's orientation period. If your management team hasn't given you the answers to these questions already as part of your orientation, then you must find them out for yourself.

Ultimately, what you are after is a sense of the value you can deliver to specific people within the organization you're trying to sell to. The more market-specific detail you can get from the person you've chosen, the better off you'll be, and the further along you will be in completing Tactic 1 of your plan.

Note: in a perfect world, you'd pose these kinds of questions to the CEO or founder of the company, but it's not always possible to set up time to meet with that person. At the very least, you should be sure you've asked your sales manager or a top performer who sells the same thing as you do for insights and advice in all of these seven areas. In addition, your company's website, public relations material, and social media materials are helpful ways to answer the questions above. Even competitors' websites may have helpful information on industry pain points and client needs.

You will be ready to reach out to prospects when you have completed Tactic 1 of the plan. Then you'll know what value you can deliver, how the best people in your organization or industry have overcome the most common objections to booking meetings to hear about that value, and the client stories that will win you credibility, attention, and interest and will give you a reason to ask for, and receive, a meeting.

INFORMATION FROM THE FRONT LINES

It would be nice if debriefing the top sales and marketing people in your organization was enough to give you all the information you need to Bulletproof yourself and your sales process. Unfortunately, that's not the case. Remember the Power of Ten: when you connect with the people inside your target organization you need to have multiple reasons for setting up a meeting with them. Most salespeople only have one reason for scheduling a meeting, and they simply repeat that same reason over and over again. That's not Bulletproofing, that's asking to fail. Doing your intelligence gathering properly means that you'll have at least 10 reasons to ask for your meeting. Therefore, in order to arm yourself with enough information, you must also find a way to talk to the people on the front line. The front line is where all the action happens. It's where the exchange of value between your company and its clients takes place.

Your next source of information is from the "front liners." Front liners could be the actual clients of your organization, or they could be people within your company who are personally responsible for implementing your company's best ideas. They might even be a third party of some kind, a consultant or vendor who knows exactly how your target company is implementing and benefiting from products, services, and solutions like yours.

It is critical that the front liner you interview not sell for a living. The front liner will have a whole different take on what's happening with your company's clients than the sales team does. That's a good thing! You need more than one perspective.

I'm not saying anything against the sales team, of course. They're focused on relationships, as they should be. They're in their own groove, and they are likely to have their own explanations for why a given account is happy or unhappy. However, most of them are, by definition, focused on selling rather than on implementation and value delivery. If you leave implementation and value delivery out of the discussion, you will be missing important pieces of the puzzle.

You must get another perspective. You must find out for yourself, from someone with first-hand knowledge, where and how the value your company sells is actually delivered. That means tracking down front liners who do not sell for your company. During my research with front liners, I also find out what kinds of discussions would motivate the CFO or COO of a Fortune 1000 company to sit down and meet with a salesperson. Why was that important? Because selling to these higher-level decision makers eventually results in much bigger deals, and in deals that close much faster than other opportunities.

Read this important point twice: Skipping the step of tracking down and talking to front liners who do not sell is one of the most common reasons for failure in the marketplace! The front line people are in constant communication with the clients. They hear all the benefits and pain points your clients are dealing with. They are an invaluable source of information.

WHO HAVE YOU TALKED TO?

When I consider taking on a new client at Gunpowderbusiness, I interview as many of the key people in the company as I possibly can. I want to interview the president and the people who make the product or service. I need to know I have real value to work with, or I turn down the work.

Once, an entrepreneur called me from a small town not too far away from where I lived. He wanted our team to book CEO meetings for him. At first, I did not take him seriously. When I visited his website, it looked like it had been created in someone's basement over a weekend. He had no corporate image, and the description of what he did was not well written. What caught my eye, though, was the fact that he had lots of great local testimonials. I was intrigued.

When I met with him, he spoke very articulately about the specific ways that he could help a CEO. He had lots of great examples and stories of the work that he and his group had done. I was almost sold on this fellow, but I told him that before taking him on I wanted to speak to three CEOs he had already helped. (I also told him that he was going to have to agree to change his image and his website. After all, a bad website makes booking a CEO meeting next to impossible!)

Three months later, he came back ready to go. When I interviewed the three CEOs he had pointed me toward, I got all kinds of great information. One of the CEOs was the head of the largest grocery store chain in the country, and the other two headed major manufacturing companies. These were big fish! I found out all the reasons these CEOs hired and kept working with my small-town fellow. He really knew his stuff. Had I not taken the time to interview those CEOs, though, I would never have been able to arm my people with the tools they needed to be successful. In his case, the knowledge transfer had to come from his own customers.

"By associating with wise people you will become wise yourself."

~ MENANDER.

A side note: later on, you will see an example of the letter we crafted for this entrepreneur and sent out via email. Through salesforce.com, we were able to confirm that the letter, which we sent to the CEO of a major fast-food chain, was circulated and opened over 200 times within the company. My point is this: if you have a well-crafted message, people are going to be interested in reading it and sharing it. However, you *cannot* create that kind of message without doing your homework.

MORE TALES FROM THE FRONT LINES

One of our early clients at Gunpowderbusiness was Cygnal Technologies, one of the fastest growing telecommunications firms in Canada. I knew absolutely nothing about telephony when I started work on that account, so I had to talk to some front liners.

In addition to interviewing their internal champions (the senior salespeople, the sales management, even some of their top executives), I also made a point of asking for the opportunity to talk to some of the people at Cygnal's most valuable accounts. I wanted to find out why they had chosen Cygnal Technologies, and just as important, why they had stayed with the company.

The VP of Marketing, Horst Schmit, told me that he had tried working with all kinds of people with the aim of helping Cygnal book meetings for their sales team; everyone had failed. He'd even tried some in-house customer service agents, thinking that if these agents knew the products well, they might be able to book meetings for salespeople. That didn't work out, either. In fact, nothing had worked thus far—because no one at Cygnal had taken the time to interview the front liners—the people who actually installed the technology at the client sites.

Even though I had no technical background in the company's offerings when I started out, I was able to uncover some incredibly valuable information: information about voice-over-IP programs, about increasing the efficiency of workgroups, about saving money by reducing long distance expenses. Soon, I was able to craft a value proposition that gave my client a competitive edge in the marketplace. As a result of that research with the front line people, my team at Gunpowderbusiness was the first successful lead generation program *ever* in Cygnal's history—and they'd been trying to generate leads for over a decade! That's the power of proper Bulletproofing.

Corporate Express was another big client of ours. When we took them on, I made sure that I interviewed all the top salespeople I could find, as well as some of their senior marketing executives. But the picture wasn't complete. I knew I still wasn't ready to try to schedule appointments with C-level decision makers at big companies. I couldn't start developing the stories and responses I would need for those decision makers until I talked to some of the people on the front line.

It wasn't until I was able to talk to an account manager who was actually responsible for implementing the Corporate Express programs at Fortune 500 accounts that I realized that what the salespeople were talking about was not what I wanted to talk about with these decision makers. By the way, this wasn't the fault of the salespeople, they'd simply been given marketing materials that didn't capture the true value that they were bringing to their best clients.

I had to talk to an account manager to learn about that value for myself. She told me all about the work she'd done at a major North American bank. She told me who the key people were in the account, what they were expecting from her, and how they were evaluating the relationship. After discussing that implementation with her in depth, I realized that what the salespeople were focused on—reducing the price of a package of pencils—had little to do with why that bank was one of Corporate Express's best customers.

What that bank was really interested in doing was eliminating maverick spending across their organization. That's where Corporate Express was really adding value. By allowing Corporate Express to come in and streamline the procurement process, set up internal controls, and assign purchasing authority to fewer people, the bank was saving literally millions of dollars every year.

These huge accounts really weren't interested in whether a package of pencils cost $1.99 or $1.89. They were interested in changing the process by which their employees received office supplies. They were interested in removing inefficiencies in the procurement process. If I had never spoken with the front liner who went into the account and figured out how to implement Corporate Express's best practices, we would have failed in our mission. As a result of doing my homework up front, Corporate Express was our client for over seven years and rolled us out in Canada and the United States, used our help to sell four other lines of business, and had us set up meetings with strategic accounts in Germany, France, England, and other parts of Europe. We helped them capture close to 90 percent of the Fortune 1000 companies in that seven-year period.

A FINAL WORD ON YOUR INTELLIGENCE BRIEFING

To recap, your intelligence briefing involves knowledge transfers from two sources:

- The very best salespeople in your organization. These people can share what they've learned about the market and what they're doing with that knowledge.

- The people on the front line. These should either be people who have personal responsibility for deploying your products, services, and solutions to clients, or the clients themselves. Front liners can share with you what value your product offers to them and how they actually use it. If you don't take the time to learn what the front line people know, you may end up selling cheap pencils when what you really should be selling is an end to maverick spending. Of those two products, which do you think a CEO or CFO is going to be more interested in talking about?

When I share with salespeople the importance of Bulletproofing, my big fear is that they're going to spend too much time doing research, and not enough time prospecting. To Bulletproof yourself, you need to learn enough about your product or service and the target organization's requirements to have intelligent, value-added, and compelling conversations with decision makers. But remember—this step is about arming yourself with good information so you can accelerate the sales process; it is not about locking yourself away, doing research, and avoiding making prospecting calls. Give yourself firm deadlines for Bulletproofing yourself. When this is done correctly, your confidence will soar as you steep yourself in the value you have to offer.

CHAPTER SIX

Tactic 1: Target Acquisition

"Audacity, audacity, always audacity!"
~ GENERAL GEORGE S. PATTON JR.,
QUOTING GEORGES DANTON

A contact you met and hit it off with at a trade show calls you with a referral: the C-level decision maker at a company that perfectly matches your ideal customer profile. You act on the opportunity immediately and quickly establish rapport with both the decision maker and the decision maker's executive assistant. On the first call, you schedule a half-hour slot to talk about whether it makes sense to meet in person. At the end of that second call, you schedule the face-to-face appointment. This scenario arises from what's called a warm lead—and most of us have a pretty good idea of what to do with warm leads. Unfortunately, we don't generally create enough of those kinds of leads to hit (or exceed) our quotas. In fact most decision makers are too busy to attend trade shows and your leads from them are often far too low on the corporate decision making ladder.

So, who do you call when you exhaust all of your warm leads? The people on your target acquisition list. (Some people call this a lead list, but I prefer my terminology, since it's focused on the goals of targeting and acquiring customers.) I believe that the quality of your performance at the end of the year—and thus, the quality of your standard of living—is directly related to the quality of your target acquisition list. The second step of the Basic Training and Reconnaissance tactic is to develop this list.

BUILDING YOUR TARGET ACQUISITION LIST

Here's how I learned the importance of the target acquisition list. When I started working at Citytv as a brand-new representative, virtually all the accounts that were currently advertising on TV were "protected." If an account was protected, it meant that a rep in the company had claimed it, and no other rep could challenge the lead for 30 days. If the rep had no traction after 30 days, you could challenge the lead...but you really didn't want to go there. Instead, you wanted to be the first one in the prospect's office. Management devised this protection list so that multiple reps would not contact the same potential customer. It covered the entire marketplace of current advertisers, and some sales executives were protecting over 300 targets. This meant that I couldn't call them.

Basically, there were no current advertisers for me to call, and hundreds of potential accounts reserved for other Citytv reps. This was not a good situation for me! I had to think outside of the box. I had to go after potential advertisers who weren't currently using television as a medium.

Since the company did not provide one, I built my own target acquisition list. I tracked down companies who were advertising in other media (typically print or radio), wrestled my way onto their calendars, and showed them a carefully crafted research presentation. My point was that by moving a little bit of money out of their print or radio budget they could reach many more people than they were currently reaching. I knew that if they tried what I was suggesting, they would reach more people— and increase their advertising spend with me. And I was right.

In a way, my success at Citytv was (at least in part) a function of the quality of the list I was willing to put together. I decided I wanted a quality list to call—so I built it for myself. I became known for successfully capturing new revenue streams from nontraditional television users like Roots Canada, Wittnauer International, Movado, Guardian Group of Funds, and many computer companies. In fact, I vertically focused and made a whole specialty out of computer and technology companies because they were new back then. What were my alternatives? Calling no one and complaining about how all the good accounts were protected?

If you are going to succeed with the Gunpowder Bulletproof Prospecting System, there are two key points to remember about target acquisition:

- You are responsible for creating your own target acquisition list—even if (especially if) management doesn't, or can't, give you good leads. It's your revenue on the line. You are the only person who is truly responsible for growing that revenue, and you are the one who has to be comfortable and confident in pursuing each and every target on that list. Whether you inherit a list or have to create one from scratch, be sure it's one you like.

- You must dream—and dream big. Think beyond what the other salespeople are going to be thinking. Make sure you are creative with at least part of your list. I didn't create a list of little print and radio advertisers. I went after major advertisers who hadn't yet moved into television. As a result, I won business that eventually turned into big accounts. I couldn't have won those big accounts if I hadn't been willing to prospect them in the first place, and I certainly wouldn't have won them if I hadn't been creative in drawing up my list.

Was it scary to target major jewellery, insurance, and financial companies? A little, but I backed up my calls, and eventually my presentations, with a lot of research. So I was Bulletproofed, and by the time I got through to a prospect, I wasn't as scared as I might have been. What was really scary was the idea of having no one to call.

Remember: if you're not scared, you're not challenging yourself. Fear can be a great motivator. It was for me.

"Fortune favors the brave."
~ PUBLIUS TERENCE

The Dream List

Now we are going to develop your target acquisition list. What kind of mindset should you have when you are putting it together? Here are a few tips for Bulletproofing your target list:

Dream Big. When you create your target acquisition list, think big. Why? Because once you run out of warm leads, you need something to do! I like to call on my dream list of ideal customers, and I like to challenge my clients to do the same. Here's what I tell them to do: make a list of the top 100 companies you would love to have on your client list. Whenever you run out of good leads from other sources, and that's going to happen a lot, call the people on your dream list.

Work from Abundance. Sometimes I meet with business owners who say they have six companies they'd like to do business with. Only having six prospects puts tremendous pressure on each interaction. Remember that one of the keys to Bulletproofing yourself from rejection is to work from abundance. If you have 100 or 1,000 prospects, then you have more opportunities for success and less pressure. So, do the research, create the value propositions, and then reach out to the people on your dream list. The way I see it, you should always have 10 to 20 people from your dream list in your pipeline. These are people who you want to turn into major customers. Once you win one as a customer, or disqualify one, find a new candidate to replace the blank spot on your dream list. Think of this list as your own personal "Most Wanted" list.

Have Quick Wins and Big Wins. Too many companies (and too many salespeople) survive on one or two large accounts; they get distracted from the essential job of creating new business relationships. For my part, I recommend that people focus on two types of accounts: quick wins and big wins. The large deals—the ones that come from the dream list—may take longer to close, but they will bring a lot of security. Quick wins are the accounts that pay the bills today, while dream list wins give you the resources to build your company for tomorrow.

Aim High! I'd much rather do the research and aim high, than try to create warm leads from things like trade shows, email, or direct marketing campaigns. There's nothing wrong with these lead sources, of course, but a key part of the strategic picture is Bulletproofing yourself by doing research on big fish so you can take advantage of those big opportunities. Most salespeople are already pretty good at aiming low, but don't spend enough time identifying potential big wins. That's why I put such emphasis on the dream list.

GET A DATA SOURCE

To build and refine your target acquisition list, you will want to start with a good data source. These days, you can buy lists very inexpensively from list brokers. Some of my favourite sources are:

- www.hoovers.com
- www.westlists.com
- www.uscompanydatabase.com
- www.jigsaw.com
- www.infocanada.ca

If you decide to buy a list, be sure you buy one that is no more than two years old. A list that is seriously out of date will cost you too much in terms of time and aggravation. Occasionally, of course, you will run into old, outdated information, no matter what list you buy; that's to be expected. Sometimes having an old name and number (from any source) can be helpful when you're trying to get past the switchboard. For instance:

Receptionist: "ABC Industries, this is Sally. How may I direct your call?"

You: "Oh, hi Sally. I must have the wrong number. I was trying to call Bob Smith, your CIO?"

Receptionist: "He left the company."

You: "Oh, who is the CIO now? Is his EA still Jennifer?"

Receptionist: "Just a minute, let me see...no, Nancy is the EA and Janet Smith is now the CIO."

You: "Do you have Janet's extension?"

Receptionist: "Yes, it's 238. I'll connect you."

LEVERAGING CURRENT RELATIONSHIPS: THE POWER OF REFERRALS

In addition to creating brand-new relationships, you will also want to leverage the relationships you already have. This is one of the very best ways to upgrade your target acquisition list. The best leads, of course, come from referrals, and my experience is that leads that come from personal referrals should always have the highest priority in terms of the actions you take on a given day.

Creating these high-value targets should be a major part of your lead development strategy. In my case, I belong to several business groups. Some of them meet once a month, and some meet weekly. I invest a good deal of time in these groups because they have become an excellent source of referrals for me.

I should acknowledge here that it took a while for the referral generation process to ramp up, but meeting with these groups on a regular basis really paid off. The members slowly learned about me and about the work I specialize in, and eventually started referring me to the people in their networks. One year I received over $250,000 in referral business from one of these groups. Clearly, that was time well spent!

Consider joining business groups such as Toastmasters, Business Network International (BNI), technical groups, boards of trade, regional groups, Rotary club, YPO, WPO, and Mastermind groups. Ask successful people what clubs or groups they belong to, and consider that there may be great opportunities to develop relationships (and help your community) by sitting on volunteer boards.

OTHER SOURCES

Other good, and inexpensive, ways to upgrade your target acquisition list are to open the local papers in your area, scan the Internet, and listen to the radio. When I worked at Citytv, I read two papers every morning and listened to the top-selling radio stations on my way to the office. Because my biggest competition, as I've already shared with you, was my other colleagues, I was constantly scanning the papers for people who were advertising in media other than television. I wanted to find new people.

Physically walking an area can be very fruitful as well. One of my colleges at Citytv saw a company called Oliver Jewellery advertising on a bus stop bench. She called him up, and that company grew into one of her largest accounts.

WHY BOTHER WITH THIS?

Many salespeople tell me that the Internet gives them plenty of leads, that they prefer to improvise when it comes to deciding whom to call next, and that they don't need a target acquisition list. I disagree—for both practical and logistical reasons. Not all business is good business. Some prospects are very profitable kinds of business, while other companies demand so much attention that they become unprofitable business. Do you know the difference yet? When I first started Gunpowderbusiness I didn't know the difference. I spoke to everyone who approached me about lead generation. After a few years I learned that some of my smaller clients where causing me the most amount of stress in my business. I remember one day when I went to visit my dentist I was stressed out and exhausted. I turned to my dentist and asked him, "How do you handle your stress?" He turned to me directly and said, "**Fire your bad clients!**" This was one of the best pieces of advice I have ever heard.

I went back to the office that day and made some changes. As a result, I was a lot less stressed out. I became more profitable and more productive and I learned to be very selective.

I encourage you to be very selective about who you put on your target acquisition list. This kind of targeted approached can save you a great deal of time and frustration.

When you set up a target acquisition list you set up a powerful goal and, like any goal that you write down and review on a regular basis, it keeps you focused and gives the laws of attraction a chance to work for you.

A WORK IN PROGRESS

I hope you've gathered by now that what I'm asking you to do is to create and refine your target acquisition list over time, rather than simply obtaining a list from a single source and marching through it blindly. The list you create and assume full ownership of is going to be indispensable as you work your way through your target organizations. I'm particularly emphatic about giving your target acquisition list a reality check by getting through to senior executive assistants, establishing a rapport with them, and finding out who the most important players are. If you don't do that, and simply go by the formal titles that show up on the organizational chart, you could wander around the corporate maze for months, or even years, without reaching the right person.

If you doubt this, consider the following list of real titles from real banks that my organization has scheduled meetings with. If we had not gotten the lay of the land from a well-placed executive assistant at each of these banks, who on earth would we have asked for a meeting?

REAL TITLES AT REAL BANKS ...
BUT WHERE'S THE RIGHT POINT OF ENTRY?

CIO; Chief Enterprise Architect; Vice President, Product Management; Product Executive; EVP Director -Call Center and Internet Channel; Retail Product Manager, Sr. Exec Mktg and CRM, International Retail Banking and Consumer Banking Management; SVP, CTO Group; Sales Process Director, SVP; Director- International Retail Bank; Executive Vice President; Enterprise Strategic Architect Financial Services; Senior Vice President - Global Marketing; Senior Vice President, Internet Strategy; Vice President - Strategic Partnerships & Channel Management; VP / Managing Enterprise Architect; AVP- Business Strategy & Implementation; VP / Operations Manager Retail Mobile Channel; Product Manager / eBusiness Consultant ; Product Manager - Home Equity Group; SVP, Product Manager;

Vice President Product Manager; Vice President, Product Manager; Senior Vice President, Internet Services Group; Chief Marketing Officer / EVP; Product Manager - Electronic Marketing and Cross Sell; President at PNC Consumer Services; V.P., eBusiness; AVP, Business Systems Analyst, Retail Internet Banking; Senior Product Manager; SVP Innovation, Research & Development; VP, Head of Consumer Deposit Products; Time Deposit Product Manager; Senior Vice President, Consumer Product Management; Mortgage Marketing Executive; VP, Contact Center Operations Executive; Vice President - Strategic Insights; SVP - Wealth Management Pricing; SVP, Deposits Balance Growth Executive; SVP, Product Delivery Manager; VP/ Home Equity Business Transformation; Checking Acquisitions Strategic Marketing Executive/SVP; Vice President Consumer Market Manager; Vice President, Merchant Service Product / Product Management Executive, SVP; Sr. Vice President, Credit Process Technology; Senior Vice President Business Intelligence; Credit Card Act Process Manager; SVP, Checking Deposits Product Manger; VP, Database Marketing; Consumer Market Executive, SVP; Senior Vice President Mass Market Strategy.

AIM HIGH!

As you develop and refine your target acquisition list, keep this in mind: I have found that salespeople trying to implement this program are willing to do everything I ask them to do—except call the executives in the organization. They'll do the research. They'll talk to the end users. They'll create the right reasons for the call. They'll do everything else I suggest. And then, after doing all that work, they sabotage their own mission by calling the wrong person! Don't just aim high in the quality of client you are looking for—aim high within the organization. It is always better to be directed down the organizational chart than up.

This is the single most likely reason for this program to fail: calling too low in the enterprise. If you want to get the results you deserve, you must reach out to the following people and continue trying to connect with them:

- C- Level Executives
- Owners
- Founders
- Senior Vice Presidents
- Executive Assistants who work for any of these people

You must avoid the temptation to reach out to the contacts you may have grown used to reaching out to: purchasing agents, front-line people, or middle management. The big deals start at the top!

When I train my own people to use Gunpowder's Bulletproof Prospecting System, I sometimes notice them reacting to calls where the person has been rude with them, hung up on them, or otherwise given them grief on the call. My question for them is always the same: "What level were you calling?"

Guess what? 99 percent of the time, they tell me it was middle management who was treating them badly! Senior executives virtually never treat people like that. It follows, then, that to properly Bulletproof yourself and your process you *must* call the right people. By reaching out to the people at the top, you'll spend a little more time, effort, and energy trying to make contact, but you'll also save yourself a great deal of aggravation.

Yes, calling low in the organization feels easy at first. The truth is, however, that it's not really easy at all. Calling low in the organization means fewer deals close. Calling low in the organization means more problems you can't solve. Calling low in the organization lengthens your sales cycle, and that means you are working harder for fewer sales.

Your own force of habit is a strong enemy here. Remember, you must exercise military-grade discipline. You must train yourself to reach out to the right people. The rewards for doing so are immense. I like to ask my clients to think of every hour of prospecting like a thousand dollars in their pocket. How many dollars do you want?

WHY CALLING THE RIGHT LEVEL IS CRUCIAL

Once you start at the level of the middle manager or the purchasing agent, you can never go over that person's head without causing political damage for yourself. However, if you start at the top, you can always go back to the person to whom that middle manager ultimately reports.

For example, I was working for a software company that wanted to win business from the cosmetics giant Avon. I targeted the senior vice president at Avon, and eventually won a meeting with him. He was a triple type A personality, the only man in 15 years of selling who made me nervous from the moment I met him. From the outset, I was stumbling over my words. I knew I only had 30 minutes on his calendar, but I simply could not get the words out.

Finally, I just stopped. I felt like this man was not going to give me the time of day.

I looked at him and said, "You make me feel really nervous." All of a sudden he changed, right before my eyes. He sat back, his body language changed, he began breathing differently, and he was receptive. This all happened in less than one minute; the energy of the meeting changed entirely. Now I was able to tell him about the great job we'd done building the Bodyshop International intranet site, which was the main parallel I'd wanted to draw during our conversation. I told him that both my president and I were certain we could do an even better job with his organization and that we were more than prepared to invest the resources necessary to meet his deadline.

Luckily for me, I convinced him of the value the software company could add to Avon. I earned a champion within the organization—and a referral to the lower-level manager who was handling the Request for Proposal (RFP) process. Let's call that mid-level manager Fred.

As it happened, Fred was not at all certain he should incorporate my company into the bidding process for the project. He had already picked his favourite vendor for the job and was merely going through the motions with the RFP. The word went out to my superiors that we were officially out of the running. And if I had begun my calling efforts with Fred, we would have been!

However, since I had started much higher in the organization, I thought I should give my new friend, Mr. Senior Vice President, an update. That got us back in the game: I left a voice mail message update with the senior vice president thanking him for the referral. I told him that I was glad to have been connected to the right person, but that Fred was skeptical about our ability to add value, while both my president and I were certain of it. Within half an hour of my leaving that message, my president called me on my cell to tell me we were back on track! He asked me what I had done to get us into this RFP, because all the senior managers had heard that Fred shut us out.

If I had not developed a friendship at the senior level of that organization, nothing good would have happened. Breaking into a closed RFP is no small feat. Did my ability to connect with senior people make me look like a star to my president? Absolutely! I was successful because I had a champion within the target company.

If you need some guidance to help you determine who is the right person to target, please review the exhibit that follows. It's a conversational "talk track" we developed in partnership with a software company to qualify suspects for meeting requests at banks in the U.S. marketplace. Use it as a model. Notice that the recommended approach is to first determine where the individual fits within the organization, and then to ask questions relevant to that organization/role. Having a great list of questions puts you in the position of power. **The person who asks the questions controls the conversation**. With that in mind prepare your list of questions in advance of picking up the phone. Your current mission: find the right decision maker!

BATTLE PLAN FOR GUNPOWDERBUSINESS SALES DEVELOPMENT MANAGERS - BANK PROJECT

WHO AM I TALKING TO QUESTIONS:

These identify the individual's role within the organization.

- What is your role within the bank?
- Are you in Marketing, Product Management, IT, or Delivery Channels? Or other?
- Who in your organization is responsible for Product Management?
- Who in your IT organization is responsible for core banking and retail delivery systems?
- Who is responsible for your retail delivery channels like Branch, Call Center, and Internet

MARKETING/PRODUCT MANAGEMENT QUESTIONS:

Ask these questions if the individual is in a product management role.

- Who owns product strategy and innovation in your organization?
- Who owns the individual lines of business such as Checking, Loans, Cards?
- What other product lines do you have?
- Are you currently satisfied with the time-to-market for your new products and product changes?
- If not, where do you see the bottlenecks/delays in getting to market faster?

Bundling use case questions

- Are you marketing any product bundles?
- If yes, have you had any challenges maintaining or updating them?
- If no, are you planning or thinking about product bundling?
- What challenges are you facing or do you foresee in rolling out bundles?

Legislative change use case questions

- Have you done anything yet in response to the coming regulatory changes in Overdraft Protection?
  - If yes – How easy or challenging was it to implement these changes?
  - If no – Are you planning any product changes in response to these regulations?
- Do you foresee any challenges implementing your planned changes?
- How will these regulatory changes impact your overall product portfolio and strategy?
- Are you concerned about loss of customers and revenue?
- Product Life Cycle Management use case questions
- Do you have a Product Development/Management process?
  - If yes – Is it a manual or automated process?
  - Is the process fast enough to respond to the needs of the business for product innovation and change?
  - If no – Why not? What are the key challenges?

- Is the current process auditable? Is that a requirement for internal compliance?

Referral questions

- Who would you suggest I speak with in your IT organization regarding rolling out product changes and updates?
- Who would you suggest I speak with in your delivery channel organization regarding sales education and readiness for product changes and updates?
- Is there anyone else in your organization I should contact?

INFORMATION TECHNOLOGY QUESTIONS:

Ask these questions if the individual works in an IT role.

- What are your priorities in the coming year related to product innovation and change within your organization?
- Do you have any Core System renovation projects underway or planned for the coming year?
- Are you facing any challenges getting product information into or out of core systems or delivery channel systems?

Legislative change use case questions

- Have you done anything yet in response to the coming regulatory changes in Overdraft Protection?
    - If yes – How easy or challenging was it to implement these changes?
    - If no – Are you planning any product changes in response to these regulations?

- Do you foresee any challenges implementing your planned changes?
- How will these regulatory changes impact your overall product portfolio and strategy?
- Are you concerned about loss of customers and revenue?

Referral Questions

- Who would you suggest I speak with in your Marketing or Product Management organization regarding product innovation and change management?
- Who would you suggest I speak with in your delivery channel organization regarding sales education and readiness for product changes and updates?
- Is there anyone else in your organization I should contact?

RETAIL DELIVERY CHANNEL QUESTIONS:

Ask these questions if the individual is in a Channel role (Branch, Call Center, Internet)

- Are you responsible for all retail delivery channels or specific channels only?
- If specific – Which channels are you responsible for?
- Who in your organization is responsible for the other channels?
- Are you facing any challenges regarding the consistency and timeliness of product information and updates?
- What are your priorities in the coming year regarding product information and updates?
- Are product information, eligibility, and other rules embedded

in your channel systems?

- What challenges do you face keeping your channel systems up to date with product information?

Legislative change use case questions

- Have you done anything yet in response to the coming regulatory changes in Overdraft Protection?
  - If yes – How easy or challenging was it to implement these changes?
  - If no – Are you planning any product changes in response to these regulations?
- Do you foresee any challenges implementing your planned changes?
- How will these regulatory changes impact your overall product portfolio and strategy?
- Are you concerned about loss of customers and revenue?

Bundling use case questions

- Are you marketing any product bundles?
- If yes, have you had any challenges maintaining or updating them?
- If no, are you planning or thinking about product bundling?
- What challenges are you facing or do you foresee in rolling out bundles?

Referral Questions

Ask these questions to determine who is responsible for X and who else you can speak to within the organization.

- Who would you suggest I speak with in your Marketing or Product Management organization regarding product innovation and change management?
- Who would you suggest I speak with in your delivery channel organization regarding sales education and readiness for product changes and updates?
- Is there anyone else in your organization I should contact?

OTHER ROLE QUESTIONS:

Ask these questions if the individual you reach is in a role other than one that's listed above.

- In your role are you concerned with or impacted by product innovation and product changes?
  - If yes – How are you impacted?

Referral Questions

- Who in your organization might be facing challenges related to time-to-market for product changes?
- Who else would you recommend I speak to about time-to-market acceleration for product changes?

I realize that this is a really complex example. The point I want you to take away is that at large organizations there are many points of entry. You need to ask lots of good questions to qualify the lead and to ensure the person you have targeted is the real decision maker. Now it's time to harness your fear, grab your target list and value propositions, and get on the phone. Just like the Gunpowderbusiness reps, your first goal will be to find the name and contact information for a target at 20 companies on your list. This will help you to fine tune your target list and is essential before you tackle Tactic 2.

CHAPTER SEVEN

Tactic 2: First Contact

"I believe in the old and sound rule that an ounce of sweat will save a gallon of blood."
~ GENERAL GEORGE S. PATTON JR.

As I mentioned in Chapter 4, your first contact with a prospect will be via a valuable, upbeat voice mail message. I know that after doing your Tactic 1 research work and honing your target list, you're probably anxious to get on the phone and reach out to your prospects, but you're not yet cleared for takeoff. Instead of beginning by calling a prospect, you'll begin by calling a colleague (or your manager) and leaving a *practice* voice mail message that draws on everything you have learned thus far. In other words, you will practice leaving a voice mail message before you actually leave one for a prospect.

When I tell salespeople that it's time to leave me a practice voice mail message, they are sometimes a little surprised. First, they haven't worked up what they feel is the "right" script yet. Second, when they do finalize that script, they expect to be able to leave voice mail messages for their real live prospects, not their manager.

Yet that's what I want them to do. Once they've done all of their intelligence gathering and used that information to identify all the right reasons for making the call, I make sure my people leave me a voice mail message first, so I can hear exactly what their message sounds like.

Just knowing what you want to say is not enough. It's also very important to know why you want to leave this message and to not sound scripted. The tonality and emotion of your voice mail message are at least as important as the content, and probably more so. You want to sound warm and approachable. (By the way, if you're not yet certain about why you're leaving this message, then you have not yet completed the knowledge transfer and value identification activities from Tactic 1; go back, do them now, and come back when you're ready to leave this message.)

READY, AIM...PRACTICE

Based on the information you uncovered about the target company during Tactic 1, I want you to call a colleague or your manager and leave your best *improvised* voice mail message. Relax, you'll learn more about scripting later. Right now, you're going to use a simple outline to practice positive emotion and tonality.

Let the colleague or manager know ahead of time that you're going to be leaving this practice message, and make sure the person lets the call go through to voice mail and then saves the message for you so you can listen to it yourself.

Remember: before you make your practice call, you must get into a positive frame of mind and body, as we discussed earlier. This is very important. As you'll recall, I used to do this by calling a friend before I made calls; you might choose to change your frame of mind and body by listening to a high-energy song or changing your physical posture. However you get yourself into a good state—you must do it! Then, pick up the phone with positive energy and a genuine smile on your face, and improvise the best voice mail message you possibly can. Remember that senior people want to interact with their peers and with people who will add value to their day. Make sure you sound like that!

Say:

- Who you are.
- The name of your company.
- Why you're calling.
- Who else your company has worked with.
- How you think you can help the person (your value proposition). Keep this short and to the point.

Then:

- Ask for the meeting.
- Leave your number *twice*.
- Promise to send an email.
- Say thank you and hang up.

DO NOT come up with an excuse for skipping this step.

CRITIQUE THE MESSAGE

After you have left the message, you must listen to it closely. This, too, is non-negotiable. Don't be surprised if you don't like what you hear. Ask your colleague or manager to listen to it, as well. Ask for constructive criticism and take notes when you get it. Figure out what you would do differently next time. If no colleague or manager is available to help you with this step, you will have to critique the message yourself. You'll be surprised how your voice sounds if you haven't listened to it on voice mail before. Don't get downhearted if you don't like what you hear, this is very valuable for your growth, and you'll sound great after practice.

This step—improvising and critiquing a practice voice mail message—is critical. Do not move on to the next step until you have completed the assignment of leaving your practice voice mail message with someone you trust and respect and then discussing what worked and what didn't work with that person.

THE FIRST (REAL) VOICE MAIL MESSAGE

Guess what? It's time to take action. By now:

- You should know three different ways to get yourself into a positive, enthusiastic, optimistic frame of mind; a frame of mind that reflects the winner you really are when you get on the phone.
- You can tell whether you're in such a state of mind or not (and thus whether you are ready to pick up the phone).
- You have your target list and your value propositions.
- You know the client testimonials that give you instant credibility.
- You know *exactly* how and where your product or service adds value.

- You've practiced and revised your voice mail message with a colleague or manager if possible, and if not, on your own.
- You've hit (or even exceeded) your first calling goal, which was to get on the phone and identify decision makers at 20 different companies and get their email address or the email address of their executive assistant
- You're comfortable making calls and interacting in a positive way with front-office people and gatekeepers.

(By the way, if any of the above is not yet true, then you are, alas, not yet ready to leave your first voice mail message. Come back to this chapter when you are ready. Remember, we don't want you doing cold calls. If you work this system properly, by the time you speak live with someone, that person will know who you are, why you are calling, and the good work you have done for others.)

THE FIRST QUESTION

The first thing people usually ask me about when it comes to leaving voice mail messages is: "What do I do if the decision maker picks up the phone and I have to talk to the person live?"

The answer is: "Relax." You don't have to worry about that right now. You're still getting used to the system. I'm going to ask you to get familiar with the process of just leaving messages for at least the first two days or so before you attempt to make any voice-to-voice contact with a decision maker.

And let's face facts—most decision makers don't pick up the phone. Getting someone live on the phone will actually be the hardest part of your mission. As a practical matter, this means that for the first few days, you will make calls when you feel relatively certain that the decision maker you're calling is not going to be there to pick up the phone. You'll only be calling new companies during regular business hours to find out who the right decision maker really is.

If for some reason you actually get a live decision maker on the phone by mistake, you will tactfully disengage from the call by saying something like, "I'm sorry, I think I've reached the wrong party."

THE SECOND QUESTION

The second thing people always ask me when it comes to leaving voice mail messages is: "What script should I use?" Personally, I always pre-ferred *not* to use a script when I made these calls.

Instead, I tried to follow a simple sequence of reminders about what is actually supposed to happen on the call. Here's a list that you might choose to post prominently in whatever space you decide to use when you place your voice mail calls:

Happy Face Positive Energy		
Why I Am Calling Credibility (Companies We've Worked With) Problems We Have Solved How We Can Help (Benefits Statement)		Ask For The Meeting
Leave Contact Number	Promise To Send Email Promise To Follow up (no specific date)	Leave Contact Number (Again)

Here's the moral: if you make sure to work all of the above into your voice mail message every time, especially the happy face and the positive energy, you'll be fine, and you really won't need a script.

Read that part again! It's important.

Ideally, you won't need to follow a script, given all the research you've done. Of course, if you really want to develop a script *and* you can deliver one without sounding like some kind of sedated android (which is how most salespeople using scripts end up sounding), you can certainly use one.

Here are some models that you can use to create your own script if you wish.

Hello, it's [name] calling from Elopa. I would like to set up a strategic meeting with you to discuss how you can improve the quality of leads your sales folks get.

Elopa is a marketing services provider that works along with your marketing department to target prospects and customers more effectively. We work with companies like Nokia, Marriott Vacation Club, Volvo, Cognos, and 100's of others who are concerned about:

- Not getting enough returns from their marketing dollars
- Not driving enough quality leads to sales
- Not able to measure the effectiveness of their campaigns

Does any of this strike a chord with you?

I'd like 15 minutes of your time to simply ask you a few questions about your marketing practices to see if there might be a strategic fit for our companies to work together.

Our marketing methodologies focus on 3 key areas:

- Increasing your marketing effectiveness.

- Helping you drive more leads to your sales team and track them

- Measuring returns from marketing dollars

Elopa has a methodology for "Optimizing Lead Generation." What's the Payback? Companies that have optimized lead generation have more sales reps meeting quotas, higher conversion and win rates, and faster ramp-up for new salespeople than their peers.

I will send you an email outlining more details and client examples of how we can help companies like yours double their sales.

I look forward to following up with you to set a time in your calendar.

Again, it's [name] I can be reached at 555-555-5555.

Have a great day!

My name is Peter Kennedy.

I'm a senior corporate-commercial lawyer with Roberts Verdon LLP, a long-established downtown law firm. Prior to joining Roberts Verdon, I was a Vice President and Division Counsel to a Fortune 100 company: ABC Industries Inc.

The reason I'm calling is that we've devised a new solution for companies that would like to obtain the benefits of having full-time in-house legal

Counsel but can't justify the cost. We are offering companies like yours the opportunity to retain our firm as in-house legal Counsel on a part-time basis.

By having your own in-house Counsel, your business would obtain the benefits enjoyed by larger corporations with full-time in-house Counsel, but at a fraction of the cost.

I wanted to call to see if there is a time when we can set up a short introductory conference call or meeting with you to discuss this new solution. Please give me a call at 416-999-9999.

I will send you an email outlining the benefits, and I look forward to following up with you in a couple of days.

Again, my name is Peter Kennedy, and I can be reached at 416-999-9999.

Here's another example, directed toward the executive assistant:

Good morning/afternoon_____, this is Ellen Smith at Capital Innovation.

I am hoping you can help direct me. I have been asked to set up an educational session with your senior management. I would like to know who at your company would be interested in learning about global best practices and compliance for capital project execution on large construction projects.

Past participants in this program include Acme International, Bravo Company, and Challenger International, each of whom has reduced assessments for noncompliance by over 80%.

> I am preparing the invitations and I would like your help in determining
> who best to invite from your company and when to schedule the meeting.
>
> Please give me a call at 416-999-9999.
>
> I will send you an email outlining the benefits, and I look forward to
> following up with you in a couple of days to determine who should be
> evaluating that email.
>
> Again, my name is Ellen Smith, and I can be reached at 416-999-9999.

More important than any sequence of words you decide to memorize is the *way* in which you leave this message. Do you sound happy, composed, calm, enthusiastic, and professional? Remember, birds of a feather flock together. Senior people want to interact with other senior people, and they are always looking for people who will add value to their day. Make sure you sound like that!

Once you're confident with your message and tone and you've practiced, you're ready to make initial contact with your targets by leaving voice mail messages for the top 20 names on your dream list.

CHAPTER EIGHT

Tactic 2: Advancing Constantly

*"I don't want to get any messages saying that we are holding
our position. We're not holding anything! Let the Hun do
that. We are advancing constantly and we're not interested in
holding on to anything except the enemy."*
~ GENERAL GEORGE S. PATTON JR.

Now that you have left the first voice mail message for the top 20 decision makers on your dream list, you'll send each of them an email message, just as you promised. We'll go over exactly what you should include in that email message in chapters 9 and 10. Before we leave the subject of voice mail, though, we need to talk briefly about your follow-up voice mail campaign.

Why? Because once you send that email, you are going to have to keep calling until you make voice-to-voice contact with the right senior decision maker. In most cases, that means turning the gatekeeper into an ally, being creative and observant about your calling times, and being willing to leave *multiple, varied* messages—with an upbeat attitude—for as long as it takes.

Ideally, you'll be able to reach the decision maker, voice-to-voice, shortly after leaving your initial voice mail message. But the reality is that this rarely happens. I've had many situations where it took me over a hundred calls to reach the right decision maker. Don't be discouraged by this. You can turn the situation into an advantage. Often when I finally got the person on the line, I heard the decision maker say things like, "So, we finally get to speak! I feel like I already know you. What's on your mind?" If you're persistent, if your tonality and your attitude are unfailingly positive, if you add some value to each message, you can get the same kind of positive response.

"In the confrontation between the stream and the rock, the stream always wins—not through strength, but through persistence."
~ Buddha

Consider the differences between the following examples. Both of them resulted in the successful completion of my mission; they just happened within entirely different timeframes. You have to be prepared for either eventuality.

61 Voice Mail Messages

I called the CIO of Philip Morris hundreds of times, and I left him over 61 messages. This took place over the course of nine months. That averaged about two voice mail messages a week. When he finally picked up the phone and we had our first conversation, he spoke to me like we were old friends, and he agreed to meet with me. My voice mail technique was so powerful and supportive that when he finally took my call, he was very receptive and gracious. He invited me to lunch in the private dining room at his corporate headquarters on Park Avenue in New York City. He invited six other senior directors to join us for that lunch (based on the email I sent him). Afterward, he personally referred me to the CIOs of Miller Beer, Kraft USA, and Kraft Canada. That's the power of leaving good voice mail!

Why would he do that for me? Because I had used voice mail properly and fearlessly, and I had kept moving forward. I prepared and practiced each voice mail message in advance. I kept him updated on the good work we had done for other CIOs and I shared some of my personality with him in a professional way that illustrated I was there to help him. Don't forget—voice mail is one of the most powerful weapons in any salesperson's arsenal. If used properly, it can move the relationship forward with every call. If you take my tips on leaving good voice mail messages, you too will learn how this medium can build and strengthen a relationship. Prospecting means fearlessly developing a meaningful relationship based on value.

Two Minutes

On the other end of the spectrum, there was a time when I called Toyota on behalf of one of my clients. The client wanted to reach the Chief Information Officer. I managed to reach the executive assistant to the president of Toyota. I told her all the good reasons I was looking for the CIO. We had a very pleasant call, and when it ended she said, "Let me call him for you."

Two minutes later, I got a call from the Chief Information Officer's executive assistant—and I booked the two hour meeting for my client. In other words, I sold the benefit of the meeting to the EA of the CEO, who then insisted that the EA of the CIO book the meeting!

You have to be ready for both ends of the spectrum. Sometimes it will be easy to get your meeting, while other times it will require persistence. Either way, you can't rest until you reach your goal—meeting with the decision makers on your dream list. Your mission is to search continually for allies and to connect with them consistently and on a person-to-person basis, to share your vision with them, and to win time on their calendar. That's what this book is all about—winning spots on the calendars of high-level people. Don't let the amount of time it takes discourage you. Also, you must not let yourself be so immobilized by fear that you abandon your objective, change it, or try to talk yourself out of it.

FIRST AND FOREMOST

Here's some "advice from the front." You will want to bear it in mind as you execute the long-term voice mail strategy that will support everything else that happens during your sales cycle.

Remember that most of the people you will be trying to get in touch with won't pick up the phone during business hours.

This isn't because they're dodging your calls or are out to make your life miserable; it's because they're decision makers, and decision makers are in meetings during the day. Shoot for early morning and after-work slots. Those are the times that are most likely to allow you to track down these hard-to-reach people. The best time to book a meeting, in my experience, is around 5:00 PM; that's when many decision makers are at their desk, catching up on email. The second best time is 7:00 to 7:30 AM.

YOUR VOICE MAIL FOLLOW UP STRATEGY

Here, then, is the sequence:

1. Leave your initial voice mail message.
2. Send your email message.
3. Try to get the person live (voice to voice) one or two days later. Aim to call when that person will be at their desk.

That's how you build momentum.

I call this initial sequence "launching the first assault." If I don't get through to my target at Step 3, then I add the person to my Hot Pad, which is a notebook where I keep information about everyone on my current "hot list."

The hot list is an offshoot of the dream list. It's composed of the dream list targets I am currently pursuing. I usually recommend that reps start their hot list with the top 20 names from their dream list. Some people can manage up to 50 at a time, but I find that calls often become mechanical when the numbers are that high. As you reach a contact live, schedule a follow-up date, or disqualify a target, you should rotate them off your hot list and add a new name from your dream list.

If I don't reach a target during the first two days, I increase the number of time slots during the day when I try to reach them. I will put on the pressure and try all hours of the day to reach the person, for two or perhaps three consecutive days. I recommend that you call block your number as you do this kind of intense calling. You do not leave a message every time you call, rather you leave a very polite, informative message once a day for two or three days. Then you switch to leaving a voice mail message no more than twice a week.

The key is to enlist help from others to see when your decision maker is likely to be available and receptive. Ask the executive assistant and other people who sit in the same area. I will even call the people in the office next to the decision maker I am hoping to speak to. I make it entertaining and light hearted. You have to be very professional with the phone, otherwise you will look like a stalker. Be respectful and smart about gathering intelligence about who makes decisions and the best way to reach them.

After that, I will continue to call, but will leave no more than two messages a week. I won't leave voice mail messages on consecutive days. I find every other day or every third day most effective for staying "top of mind" with the decision maker I'm targeting. Timing is everything in prospecting, and frequency is a big part of improving your timing. If you wait for five days between "touches," people may forget your voice mail message and your email altogether.

More About Your Hot Pad

Your Hot Pad contains your short-term target list (hot list) of the companies you just launched an assault on. It should contain name, title, company, and any information you need for quick reference. Once you add someone to this list you call the person whenever you have a free moment. Eventually, you become so focused on this list that, after a week, you can look back at the Hot Pad and get excited, because you can see for yourself how many of those people you booked meetings with.

I carry my Hot Pad around with me everywhere I go. It's always within easy reach—next to my bed, in the car, in between flights, everywhere. It's a great resource for calling people off-hours, which is what you're going to have to do in the days after you send your email message. After the initial assault, you're going to make a serious follow-up assault. The moment someone goes into the Hot Pad, I think, "This person is mine!"

As I have said, booking great senior-level meetings is a skill, one you can strengthen. You strengthen this skill with practice. One of the reasons my success ratio is so high is that my confidence gets stronger every time I cross someone off my Hot Pad and add another short-term target to replace it.

One woman on my team programs her hot list into her phone so she can speed-dial targets in between her other activities. That works for her, but I think the great thing about a paper-based Hot Pad system is that you never lose the data. Even if your computer freezes up, your data vanishes, or your battery runs out, you can still make your most important calls. In fact, it's great to use different phones when you're on the road because your caller ID will be different.

SUCCESSFUL VOICE MAIL FOLLOW-THROUGH

You must continue to Bulletproof yourself throughout the follow-through process. Vigilance is key! Do *not* expect anyone to call you back, **EVER**. This is an essential part of setting yourself up for success. Accept ahead of time that most people will never call you back. That's the reality: they won't. Real decision makers are super busy and stressed. A million people want their time. If you get a call back, that's great; take it as a bonus, but don't count on it. And whatever you do, don't act like you have a return call coming. Anyone who leaves any variation of, "I left you a message, but you didn't return my call," in a voice mail message deserves to have his or her selling license revoked—and deserves to get a boot in the bum, as well!

Vary your calls, and make sure every message you leave comes from a place of service. For instance: "I know you're an extremely busy person. I was just trying to reach you to personally book some time in your calendar to discuss X, Y, and Z benefits, which I think might fit well with your company since ABC company had such a positive experience..." The subtext of your message should always be: "I want to add value to your day and you can count on me to help you."

Use a script if you want, but make sure you never sound scripted. This point is so important that I must emphasize it again: your primary goal is to sound smart, confident and enthusiastic, as though you're inviting someone to a party. Try using bullet points if the script doesn't deliver the tone of confidence you need. And keep leaving practice messages for your colleagues and yourself to help you build confidence and continually improve your technique.

"Make a game of finding something positive in every situation."
~ BRIAN TRACY

Remember the principle of working from abundance. Aim high, but keep your targets realistic. Keep filling your sales funnel, keep calling new companies, and keep building new relationships with assistants. You should always have at least 20 to 40 names of new decision makers to call at all times, and you should have 10 to 20 people on your hot list at all times.

Strive to make the executive assistant your ally. It's your job to get the decision maker or the decision maker's assistant on the phone and to find out whether your good reasons for meeting resonate with one of them. Statistically, you're more likely to connect with the executive assistant first, so make sure your contact with this person is a positive one. That last point is particularly important—remember my call to Toyota?

CHAPTER NINE

Tactic 3: Electronic Warfare

*"Play to win at all times. I wouldn't give a hoot in hell
for a man who lost and laughed."*
~ GENERAL GEORGE S. PATTON JR.

The next phase in the Gunpowder Bulletproof Prospecting System involves creating the right email message, which is the critical link in your whole campaign. If your email message is effective, it will be focused on the moving target it must hit: the scheduled meeting with the decision maker. If your email message isn't effective, you will remain on the outside looking in.

Remember, your voice mail message must reference the fact that this email message is coming; your contact, and/or your contact's assistant, must not only be aware of its arrival, but also a little curious about what it might contain. In order to gain visibility, traction, and the appointment with the top decision maker you have targeted, you must exceed expectations and set yourself apart from the competition with this email message. That means you must go into appropriate detail in the body of the message.

I realize that this advice conflicts with the core principle of many self-appointed "experts" on the topic of C-level selling. They will tell you that senior executives are extremely busy people and, therefore, you must compress all your electronic communications to them into concise one-sentence executive summaries if you wish to hold their attention. These "experts" will also tell you that if your message requires more than one computer screen's worth of space, it will be ignored.

They are wrong.

"Email, instant messaging, and cell phones give us fabulous communication ability, but because we live and work in our own little worlds, most of that communication is totally disorganized."

~ MARILYN VOS SAVANT

As long as you use all of the research you have done up to this point to tie your message directly to the senior executive's hot buttons, you can, and should, expect the CEO and/or the assistant to keep reading. Yes, the executive is busy. What that means is that he or she will be eager to disengage from communications, in any medium, that don't support his or her priorities. If you use the information you have uncovered about the specific value your product or service delivers to people who share key concerns with the executive you are targeting, that executive will keep reading. These people did not reach the positions they now occupy by overlooking important details. They don't want to look foolish inviting people to join them at this important meeting. Give them the facts in enough detail to captivate them!

The ultimate test of your email message's viability is whether the executive assistant who supports the person you're trying to meet is as motivated as you are to get the C-level person to read what you've written. Although I don't want you to make the mistake of believing that there's a single template you can use for all of your email communications (there isn't!), I do want you to return frequently to the Harley-Davidson example that follows. Compare its tight focus and clear benefit statements to anything you write in support of the voice mail message you leave for a prospect.

None of the phases I've been sharing with you operate in isolation. When you use them, you will find that they overlap and intersect. What follows is a true story which gives you a good example of the best way to deploy all the tools I've shared with you thus far. Tools to help you expand into the realm of email communication, and to set yourself up to secure the appointment. Please note: it's much more important that your initial phone and email contact with the organization feel, more or less, like the story I'm about to share with you, than it is for you to copy the words verbatim (for either a phone script or sample email) when you reach out to a target organization.

A SUCCESS STORY TO SPARK YOUR INTEREST

An old friend of mine ran a manufacturing company in Toronto. It was quite successful, and eventually he sold that company and moved to California. His entrepreneurial impulse refused to die, however. One day, he called me up and said, "Christine, I've got a great new design for a spark plug—can you help me to figure out how we should be marketing it?"

I was happy to talk to him over the phone, and together we developed some initial ideas about what companies he should be targeting and how he should approach them. A week or so later, he called me up again. He asked me: "Christine, do you think you can get us into Harley-Davidson?"

I said, "Of course. Getting people into places is what I do!"

I told him I was going to need a couple of things from him: a little more information about him and a list of the most compelling benefits of using the spark plug. He sent me some information, and I got to work. By the time we were done, I had a series of bullet points that I could use as the outline of a game-changing voice mail message.

Those core bullet points, which were more memory joggers to me than anything else, read like this: (Which one of these points builds credibility? Answer all of them.)

- Details of the company history
- Three patents
- Tested on Harley-Davidson motorcycles
- 5 to 10% more power and torque

- 30% lower emissions
- Better fuel economy
- Great sexy sound

I had my bullet points, but I wasn't ready to make my calls yet. First, I did my research, and I identified the names and titles of three different potential decision makers within Harley-Davidson. One of these was a senior vice president. I discovered his name and I also found out the name and email address of his executive assistant.

My first call was to this executive assistant, whose name was Lori. I left her an impromptu—not scripted!—voice mail message, using my core bullet points.

In that voice mail message, I mentioned that I was doing a favour for a friend and asked if she would be so kind as to **help me** get an important email message about a high-performance spark plug to the right person within the organization. At the end of that voice mail message, I promised to send Lori an email message and then follow up by phone afterwards.

Here is the email message I sent Lori:

Hi Lori,

Can you please direct me to the right person who would evaluate a new high performance spark plug?

Multispark, LLC was formed to design, manufacture, license, market, and sell a new type of high performance spark plug, which produces multiple simultaneous ignition events from a unique firing cap. Multispark has three patents, which it licenses from its partners, and a trade secret on the assembly. The company has a trademark on the PowerSTAR brand name.

The spark plug utilizes a unique star shaped electrode made of nickel alloy that is extended to the top of a standard copper core spark plug center electrode. The shape, metal mix, and difference between the metals cause the spark plug to generate multiple simultaneous ignition events that produce a larger and faster flame front. This flame front ignites more of the fuel in the cylinders, which produces more power, torque, lower emissions, and better fuel economy.

The product has been tested extensively in Harley-Davidson motorcycles. It produces between 5-10% horsepower and torque improvements in Evolution, TC-88, and TC-96 engines.

The design and shape of the star electrode on the spark plug does not require gapping or indexing. It lasts longer, reduces fouling, starts more easily, and provides better throttle response than conventional standard spark plugs.

The spark plug has been shown to improve power over Screamin' Eagle spark plugs. Another feature of the spark plug is that it changes the sound of a fuel injection engine to a lower, deeper, throatier sound—closer to that of a carbureted engine.

Thank you for your time.

Sincerely,

Christine Aquin Pope

President & CEO

Gunpowder Business Development Inc.

www.gunpowderbusiness.com

Gunpowder Business is a team of vertical sales professionals generating truly qualified C-level leads and securing and managing sales appointments for you

Are you starting to see how all of this is coming together?

Here's the best part of the story. That day Lori forwarded my email message to the right person within Harley-Davidson, and the very next day I got an email message back from that executive telling me our timing was perfect, because Harley-Davidson was now looking for a high-performance spark plug! My friend got the meeting.

Did you spot everything that happened? You've just seen how powerful, and how fast, the system I am sharing with you in this book can be. I love this story, not just because it involved helping a friend get into a major deal, but because it encapsulates so many of the lessons I've been sharing with you in this book. Did you notice how I only had to complete phases 1, 2, and 3 in order to achieve success? My research was in depth, my voice mail message was appropriate and added value, and my email message was effective. Therefore, I never had to employ phase 4 of the Gunpowder system—voice-to-voice combat. The prospect was so impressed and interested, that he contacted me. I hope the lessons found in the previous chapters will eventually become second nature to you. Did you notice them as they zoomed by on that big, fat Harley?

Here they are again:

1. Do the research. I connected all the dots before I picked up the phone. I wasn't talking in generalities; I had identified specific benefits that were likely to be of interest to the senior-most people at Harley-Davidson. As a result, when people heard my voice mail and saw my email, they were *not* afraid to pass it along to the C-level people I was trying to contact. The email added value to the company. Most people won't pass on an email if it makes them look bad at work.

2. Call high. I didn't start by reaching out to Purchasing or Procurement. I called the office of a C-level contact. (In fact, I had three C-level contacts to choose from.) As a result, the sale accelerated from zero to sixty in a matter of seconds, just like a good Harley should.

3. Use the right tonality. The voice mail message I left wasn't a desperate plea for help; it was a request for a professional courtesy, from the office of one professional to another. I never pretended to be anyone other than who I actually was. I never came across sounding like someone who had to close the sale in order to make the mortgage payment. I sounded like what I was—the owner of my own company. Every salesperson on earth is, at the end of the day, the president of a company called Me, Incorporated, but unfortunately not every salesperson sounds like that. Remember: birds of a feather flock together.

4. Leave a powerful voice mail message first; one that concludes with a promise to send an email, and then send the email. I did what I said I was going to do. Notice, too, that I didn't dig myself into a scheduling hole by saying, "I'll call you at 8:00 AM on Monday." If you do make a commitment, keep it. Small things build trust.

5. Go into appropriate depth in your email. I know this is a compli-

cated and controversial subject, but what I want you to notice is that the email I sent was not two sentences long. Equally, it was not longer than it needed to be—it was focused on value. It detailed all the benefits I had identified in a compelling and straightforward way. That's why it got forwarded as fast as it did; that's why it produced a response as fast as it did.

6. Last but not least, turn the executive assistant into an ally. Most salespeople treat gatekeepers like enemies. I didn't, and the results speak for themselves. I asked respectfully for the assistant's **help** in passing along an important message. Isn't that what we all should be doing?

"No one who achieves success does so without acknowledging the help of others. The wise and confident acknowledge this help with gratitude."

~ AUTHOR UNKNOWN

That last point may be the ultimate lesson from the Harley-Davidson story. Most salespeople would dramatically improve their income picture if they simply started treating executive assistants as the essential players they are. To reinforce that essential point, I'd like to share a joke I came across on the Internet:

THE CANNIBALS

Not long ago, a Fortune 500 corporation hired several cannibals. "You are all part of our team now," said the HR manager during the orientation session. "You will get all the usual benefits, and you can go to the cafeteria whenever you want for something to eat, but please don't eat any of the other employees." The cannibals promised they would not.

A few weeks later the cannibals' boss remarked, "You're all working very hard, and I'm satisfied with you. However, one of our executive assistants has disappeared. Do any of you know what happened to her?" The cannibals all shook their heads, "No," they said.

After the boss left, the leader of the cannibals said to the others angrily, "Right, which one of you idiots ate the executive assistant?"

A hand rose hesitantly in admission. "You fool!" said the leader, "For weeks we've been eating managers and no one noticed anything, but nooo, you had to go and eat someone important!"

Samples of Successful Emails

Following are examples of effective email communications with C-level people. Each of them was extremely effective when it came to generating attention, interest, dialogue, and appointment commitments within the target organization. The industries in which they originated are not what matters; what matters is their relevance to the target reader.

Again, please *do not* try to copy these emails verbatim; *do* try to model their specificity, their appeal to documented facts, their use of only relevant details, client testimonials, and their call to action. Notice that each of these emails has a clear objective: schedule time to talk to me!

Dear [Name],

At Top Flight Market Intelligence, we help our clients sleep better by answering the burning questions that can keep them up at night. Questions like, "We have a strategy for growing our market share, but is it the right strategy?" We can put your mind at ease by providing breakthrough insights with actionable recommendations based on scientific research, so you can make decisions with confidence.

You may have the same questions as many of our clients:

• How do we talk to our customers more effectively?

• What new products are they looking for?

• Why do they leave us for the competition?

• What is the most effective way to get this to market?

Based on solid research we get you closer to your customers, competitors, and channel partners. We do more than just answer these questions. We develop a plan that puts you ahead of your competition and puts this information to work for you—and your bottom line.

But don't take our word for it. Here are comments from a few of our clients:

"Top Flight provided us with actionable channel intelligence and exceeded our expectations by delivering a go-to-market plan in four weeks." Jon Smith, Vice President, Commercial Development, Cellular Inc.

"We found Top Flight to be customer-focused, very knowledgeable, thorough and realistic." Paul Smith, VP Bank of America

> *"We were looking for a firm that would ask the right questions and get the information that would double our business. We actually looked at three firms. Top Flight had the best proposal and the best techniques for collecting the information from the market."* Brian Smith, Walmart Inc.
>
> We would like to introduce ourselves to you and your team, get to know your business, and understand your most critical questions. We will contact you this week, or please call us at 555-555-5555 to set up a meeting. Let us show you how our expertise can help you sleep better at night.
>
> Sincerely,

RECRUITMENT AND OUTSOURCING EMAIL

Note the use of the endorsement quote at the beginning of the message. Whenever possible, I like to use client quotes as benefits. I like doing this especially if your topic is very competitive or you simply don't have a lot of referenceable accounts.

> *"With the Maxwell HR process...we see great benefit in having a proactive, ongoing, strategic recruiting partner that will help us improve our quality of hire and reduce recruitment costs."* - A. Johnson, National Recruitment Manager for a Global Professional Services Organization

Dear John,

Successful companies of all sizes are realizing the benefits of outsourcing their recruitment functions. With Maxwell HR Outsourcing Recruitment Solutions, our goal is to revolutionize the recruitment industry with our innovative solutions. Developed over years of research and testing, our approach can help your company improve access to top talent, reduce time to hire, and increase employee retention—all while saving you money.

As your strategic business partner, Maxwell HR assigns your company a dedicated Recruitment Solutions Assistant (RSA). Working closely with your hiring team at your location, we take a proactive approach to recruitment, developing internal processes not found in traditional search firms. This allows us to deliver service that exceeds our customers' expectations.

"We have been delighted at the way Maxwell HR employees have embraced our technology and processes. They adapt their approach to suit our needs, without ever compromising their standards for 'best-in-class' mindset." - Mike Cartell, President, Graphite Technologies Inc.

Working on-site gives your RSA unique insight into your company culture. When combined with our industry leading competency and performance-based interviewing techniques, we can ensure that only the candidates best suited to your organization are selected, leading to improved employee retention.

"[Maxwell HR has] an excellent ability to identify and provide people who have the right technical skills in addition to having the right cultural fit for our

organization." - Sandra Dixon, Director, Human Resources

The innovative recruitment solutions developed by Maxwell HR can have a positive impact on your bottom line. If your company is planning to hire six or more employees in the next year, we can save you money—25% or more over traditional recruiter costs. Our model is also completely scalable, and can adjust to your ongoing recruitment needs.

"Maxwell HR offered a creative fee structure that saved us about 25% compared to typical agency fees." - Nicholas Duncan, National Recruitment Manager for a Global Professional Services Organization

Let us show you how your organization can recruit better and spend less. I will contact you this week to discuss the many benefits and outstanding value your company will realize with the leading-edge recruitment solutions offered by Maxwell HR. You can also reach me by phone at 416-999-9999 or email me at...

Sincerely,

Signature with contact information

FACILITY SUPPLIES EMAIL

Note the guarantee in the opening paragraph.

Dear Gregg,

I am writing to let you know about our breakthrough program change in the janitorial and facility supplies industry. This program can provide your organization with guaranteed savings—a minimum of 18% off your current program.

ABC Co., Inc. is a $5 billion dollar office product, service, and supply company. We have created a new national business unit—our Facility, Cleaning, and Break Room program offering. This business unit (managing sales of over $400 million by the end of this year) is specifically focused on supporting commercial customers with the products required to clean and maintain their buildings and facilities.

With our size and buying power, ABC Co. can provide savings and services that our competitors are unable to match. This is why major companies such as Microsoft, ADP, Neiman Marcus,and US Bank chose us as their national janitorial and facility supply strategic partner.

This is what makes ABC Co. the preferred choice:

- Massive buying power and direct manufacturing relationships, which drive down pricing and ensure faster product delivery to us—and you.

- National coverage to all locations in the U.S. All other vendors are regional and do not have the fleet we do.

- Next business day delivery on urgent and key items such as paper towels, trash can liners, tissue, and cleaning supplies. Our competitors average 3-5, or even 7, days to deliver these products.

- Simple-to-use Internet ordering, online billing and reporting functionality. Over half of our customers order this way. We are also fully integrated with the top E-procurement providers. Our competitors typically only offer phone or fax ordering, which are time consuming and error prone.

- One operating system, which means consistent products, packaging, billing, and reporting solutions—no matter how large, small, or far away your company or organization may be. We are the only supplier offering this.

- No minimum charges. Reduce your space consumption by buying less at one time.

Some of our major suppliers for this program include: Kimberly Clark (papers), Georgia Pacific (papers), Pitt Plastic (can liners), Johnson Diversity (chemicals and cleaners), Rochester Midland (chemicals), and 3M (chemicals, abrasives, and pads)

We would like to schedule an appointment with you to discuss how ABC Co. can help you streamline your services and save hundreds of thousands of dollars, as well as answer any questions you might have in regard to specific suppliers or programs that are of interest to you.

The ABC Co. commitment to you is that if we cannot deliver significant savings, we will not ask for your business. We look forward to further discussing this program value proposition with you.

Sincerely,

Signature with contact information

NETWORK COMMUNICATIONS EMAIL

The news brief at the beginning of the message keeps the reader scrolling down. Also note that after my signature, contact information, and the credibility piece on the company, I put a list of 20-plus current clients for the reader to review.

Lanyard Ranked Second Fastest Growing Company in the World

Monday March 4, 2002,

Lanyard Technologies Corporation (TSE:LTC), Canada's leading communications network service provider, has been ranked as the second fastest growing company in the world by PROFITguide.com, the business resource for Canadian entrepreneurs.

Dear Bill,

RE: "How A Little Strategic "Re-Thinking" Of Your Current Technology Infrastructure Today Can Deliver Big Gains In ROI, Capability, and Performance Tomorrow!"

When yesterday's network infrastructures were designed, no one dreamed of what they would be able to accomplish today. But, with a little strategic re-thinking, your existing infrastructures can reach new heights of capability and performance.

With a free Consultative Systems Audit, you can quickly and easily determine the best and most cost-effective ways to:

- Leverage current technology investments and realize quick, short-term ROI

- Facilitate a powerful migration to a converged network

- Provide mobile communications to customers or employees anywhere in the world

- Get the right message to the right customer at the right time

- Generate more up selling and cross selling possibilities

- Build and enhance intelligent call processing capacity

- Develop, expand, and deliver mission-critical networking

- Lower the total cost of ownership—your infrastructure and applications will run in a more efficient, streamlined, and cost-effective manner.

Perhaps now the timing is right to do some strategic re-thinking of your technology infrastructure. I will call you shortly to arrange a mutually convenient time to (speak, meet) to explore this possibility.

Bill, I look forward to discussing your business strategy, corporate objectives, and how we can assist Company in gaining a superior market advantage through an enhanced, integrated telecommunications solution.

Sincerely,

Signature with contact information

P.S. For practical, real world insights you can use immediately for "Surviving The High Tech Squeeze", click to http://www.lanyardbusiness.com/surviving

----

Lanyard Technologies, a publicly traded company (TSE-LTC), is involved in advanced wired and wireless high-speed networks.

Founded in 1996, Lanyard Technologies Corporation is Canada's leader in the design, integration, and management of wired and wireless broadband, data, and telecommunications networks. These networks allow Lanyard clients -- cable companies, telephone companies, broadcasters, utilities, and many others -- to communicate effectively and economically. The Company has expertise in all communications technologies including satellite, coaxial cable, fiber optics, twisted pair, and microwave.

For more than 14 years, Lanyard has been providing telecommunication solutions to organizations of all types and sizes. With over 150 professionals in 10 offices across Canada, Lanyard's national presence ensures effective personal service for all sizes of businesses right across the country.

Lanyard's integrated approach provides customers with direct access to a growing number of products and services through a single point of contact. This is accomplished via the full range of system platforms from Avaya, Cisco Systems, Syntegra, Spectralink, and Polycom.

PARTIAL CLIENT LIST

MANAGEMENT CONSULTING EMAIL

This message was read over 200 times by senior executives at one of the largest fast-food operations in the world. It's one of my favourite types of email letter. If my client has marquee clients who will give generous testimonials, I like to lace a letter with client quotes. Of course, we've changed all the names, but believe me—the big brand names made my small town fellow really stand out from the crowd.

Dear Tom,

In today's market, the pressure to outgrow and outperform the competition increases daily. As a leader, the responsibility to achieve business goals, meet key performance indicators, and exceed shareholder expectations lies squarely on your shoulders. But what if you and your team are already working to capacity? How can you lead them to the next level of success as a cohesive team without making real changes? The answer is—you can't. Even the country's leading management knows that in order to enable your team to outperform your competitors, you'll need enhanced competency, clarity of strategic vision, organizational alignment, and sustainable operational efficiency. And these aren't just buzzwords; they are the very cornerstones of any profitable corporate entity.

It's for this essential competitive advantage that companies turn to Smart Consulting.

"Smart Consulting *is ultimately creating a strategic advantage within the Acme organization by making us more efficient, quicker to the decision making, better executors, better at delivering against objectives, and that's something we need vitally.*" - Mike Dorris, Acme Worldwide

Smart Consulting is a different kind of management consultancy. With a committed, hands-on, and highly results-oriented approach, they have developed a devoted following with North American companies—large and small. In fact, 95% of our existing business is referral based. And that's because Smart Consulting gets results—faster, measurable, sustainable, and profitable results.

"I went outside the organization for help and engaged Smart Consulting *now for our shareholders, we have been able to identify $4-5 million dollars in incremental revenue. We also have implemented expense controls that will* *put at least $500,000 to the bottom line. Profitability is up 10%."* - Marjorie Powell, CEO, CorrectPoint

In a personalized process geared towards achieving your specific business objectives, Smart Consulting guides you through defining and aligning goals, facilitating and designing managerial processes, improving leadership, and establishing accountability. With a newly elevated standard of organizational focus and self-sufficient, sustainable internal competency, your company will experience an invigorated culture of clarity and determination that will allow you to grow more efficiently, achieve more effectively, and ultimately succeed faster than the competition.

With a short meeting, we can establish how Smart Consulting can help your organization to thrive, meet upcoming challenges more effectively, increase the bottom line, and instill permanent management behaviors that will power your success for years to come. With your guidance, we can customize a process to meet your business objectives, organizational requirements, and budget. And the Smart Consulting process is a permanent one—our ultimate success being your complete self-reliance.

"After working with Smart Consulting, there is an unbelievable sense of freedom and peace of mind. *I can go about my business fully confident that everyone here knows what needs to be done, and is doing their absolute best day-in and day-out, because they believe it is the best thing for them. As the leader, that removes a tremendous burden from me, and from my management team. I sleep well at night. It wasn't always like that."* - Bart Green, CEO of Beverly Group

Let us help you achieve the peace of mind that comes with knowing you're not only empowering your organization to succeed, you're getting them there as a team, and faster.

Bernice Walters will be calling you shortly to discuss scheduling an appointment. In the meantime, to learn more about what we do or hear from our clients please visit www.smartconsulting.com.

Sincerely,

Signature with contact information

FINAL THOUGHTS ON ELECTRONIC WARFARE

I would like to leave you with this essential, non-negotiable principle about the composition of email messages for C-level prospects: they take time to create and customize. Make sure you put time and effort into composing a clear and compelling customized and personalized email explaining your value proposition to each target.

The person reading the message must conclude something like this: "Wow, whoever sent us this put a lot of work into it." If you simply try to bang out a template that looks like it required five or ten minutes of your time, and just fill in the blanks for each new prospect, you will not get good results from your campaign.

There is no template. There is only a standard: is this message so closely tied into the decision maker's business that his or her assistant wouldn't dream of deleting it?

To make sure that happens:

• Lace your message with credibility: use multiple client testimonial quotes if possible. (Gather testimonials from clients continually through successive interviews.)

- Remember an endorsement quote is a particularly powerful way to open the message.
- Ask yourself: "Do all the client testimonials I am offering map back to my reader's needs? Do all of my benefit statements connect to my prospect's assumed needs?"

Remember that you're following this process of conducting proper background research, leaving an appropriate, value-added voice mail message, and sending a follow-up email so that by the time your prospect talks to you live they know why you're calling and they know the good work you have done for others. If you Bulletproof yourself properly, it's not a cold call; it's a gold call!

In the next chapter, I'll share some secrets on the effective use of another important weapon in your electronic arsenal: the email attachment.

CHAPTER TEN

Tactic 3: The Art of the Attachment

"If a man has done his best, what else is there?"
~ GENERAL GEORGE S. PATTON JR.

A perfect email is not perfect unless it has a perfect attachment. Forgetting this is the modern sales equivalent of falling asleep on the job. Don't follow up your voice mail message by sending out an email without the right attachment!

When I started working with DWL, a software company specializing in the insurance industry, I would call C-level people for months, trying to set up an appointment. Then I would finally reach the person, and my target would get rid of me by saying, "Send us a package with all of your information." That was a roadblock!

I quickly learned to send the package at the same time I sent my email. That way, I wouldn't lose a week while people were waiting for the information (and, in all likelihood, forgetting all about our call). This was a long time ago—back in the days when the idea of sending a sharp-looking digital brochure or some other piece of presentable marketing material along with an email message was still a dream.

Now that dream is an everyday reality, and the PDF attachment you send with your email message has an important strategic dimension within your sales cycle. Just as the body of your email message should "warm people up" and make them more receptive to voice-to-voice contact with you, your attachment can lend a great deal of credibility to your request for a meeting.

CASE STUDIES AS ATTACHMENTS

My preferred approach is to send, as an attachment, a compelling case study whose solutions closely match up with the challenges faced by the prospect. Case studies, by the way, have incredible power to level the playing field a small business shares with its larger competitors; when the case study is put together intelligently, it can instantly put you in the same league with much better-known competitors.

Here's an example of a case study I developed for our company. Pay particular attention to the number and the placement of the client quotes. Nothing helps to build credibility faster than the good things your clients say about you. I encourage you to take the time to develop them. They are worth their weight in gold to your future prospecting activities.

GUNPOWDER CASE STUDY:

IntelliResponse Grows from Zero to Top 3 in U.S. Marketplace

"As a young company with an unknown brand, we were trying to grow but didn't have the expertise to manage a lead generation program in-house. But we truly believed that if we could just demo our product to the right decision makers, we could win. Gunpowder was able to build and refine a prospect list for us and manage the whole process to get to that critical first meeting. With them, we were able to significantly improve the productivity of our sales force."

-Ted Madden, COO, Comtext Systems

IntelliResponse, created by Comtext Systems, is an advanced self-service information retrieval system designed to help websites respond to information requests more efficiently and effectively. The product allows users to "ask" questions online in everyday language—complete with spelling mistakes, acronyms, slang, and other anomalies. IntelliResponse then provides correct answers in real-time, thereby drastically minimizing the need for email or call centre communication. For those users requiring more support, IntelliResponse also provides a transition channel from self-service to assisted service for one-on-one communication support.

The Story

In a continual race with U.S. competitors, Canadian-based Comtext Systems knew they'd have to make some changes to their sales process in order to cross the finish line first. They had infiltrated a few U.S. Universities with IntelliResponse, but wanted to both expand within the sector and go after the difficult-to-crack U.S. Banking sector as well. The final challenge was how to get their growing sales force up to speed faster—with less time devoted to product learning and prospecting and more time spent selling and closing! Based on a referral from a former Gunpowderbusiness client, Comtext COO Ted Madden engaged Gunpowder for a 4-month pilot targeting U.S. Universities.

The Work Begins

One of the deciding factors in choosing Gunpowder was their extensive technology background. The Gunpowder team quickly grasped the software attributes and translated them into clear benefits for their target list. The knowledgeable reps were then able to discuss the product professionally with senior admissions executives.

Utilizing their unique process involving lead qualification, multiple contact points, and tenacious follow-up, Gunpowder not only established a long list of qualified prospects, but also booked an average of 12 senior-level meetings per month. The final stage constituted effectively managing the meeting process to ensure the Comtext sales team got in front of their targets quickly.

The Engagement Grows

At the end of the 4-month trial, Comtext was more than happy with the results. So much so that with great confidence it extended the University trial and added several seats to take on the challenging U.S. Banking sector.

Gunpowder identified several major roadblocks in the banking industry. First there would be the challenge of tracking down the key decision makers within these mammoth organizations, and then the challenge of convincing them to share enough information to qualify them as prospects. With their deep knowledge of the banking sector, Gunpowder went after the smart money, focusing on call center executives and retail banking executives, all for whom a reduction in center calls would mean massive savings. The second target was retail executives responsible for traditional branch networks—an environment that would additionally benefit from IntelliResponse's intranet functionality.

Testing More Waters

Based on their success, Comtext decided to use Gunpowder to test the viability of IntelliResponse in the Utilities market. Gunpowder booked over 30 meetings within a 6-week period, allowing Madden to get a close-up look at whether he should be adapting his product for that sector.

In addition, Gunpowder engaged in a research study on behalf of Comtext, assessing whether Universities were using a competitive product to IntelliResponse and, if so, determining their degree of satisfaction. This also helped to generate a new qualified target list for further calls.

The Results Are In

The IntelliResponse project has been an unequivocal success. After a two-year engagement, Comtext is now operating at such a volume that, using the best practices developed for them by Gunpowder, they've been able to move their prospecting in-house.

"There's no question that we've been able to build our market share faster with Gunpowder's help. When we started, we had absolutely no presence in the U.S. Universities market. Now we're one of the top three suppliers—and the likelihood is that we wouldn't have been able to get there without Gunpowder."

-Ted Madden, COO, Comtext Systems

"We were so impressed with Gunpowder's results, from the quality of the people we were meeting to the quality of that first call, that we had great incentive to extend the trial."

-Ted Madden, COO, Comtext Systems

"We had a list of 10,000 prospects, each with up to 8 to 10 different decision makers. With limited knowledge of those decision makers and the market in general, we needed some expert help to get us through it. We chose Gunpowderbusiness because they had real expertise in the hi-tech market and came highly recommended by a business associate who had used them with good results."

-Ted Madden, COO, Comtext Systems

"One of the key differences with Gunpowder is that over 90% of the meetings they booked for us actually took place as scheduled. And they got us in front of the right decision makers on a timely basis. This significantly improved our preliminary meeting success rate and represented a major productivity hit for our sales organization."

-Ted Madden, COO, Comtext Systems

> "By having Gunpowder test the Utilities market, we learned that it just wasn't ready for us yet. This was actually good news, because once we understood this, we were able to delay our entry into the market, saving ourselves significant time and cost. For a small company like us, this was a powerful benefit!"
>
> -Ted Madden, COO, Comtext Systems

When we interviewed our client for the IntelliResponse case study, we had all our questions lined up in advance. We wanted to tell a story of how and why he came to us. We had a goal in mind. We know that every prospect who comes to us is asking themselves the same question: "Can I trust this company to talk to C-level decision makers on our behalf?" Of course, this requires a huge leap of faith. Our goal for the case study was to tell the story of how we won Ted's confidence.

Just as we did, you must first decide what story you want to tell. What kind of narrative will resonate with your prospects? Then you must create the questions whose answers will help you to tell that story.

Here are some of the questions we asked Ted:

- Why did you choose Gunpowder?
- What did you feel were the greatest challenges you needed Gunpowder to help you overcome?
- Did Gunpowder effectively deal with these challenges? How?
- In simple terms, describe the work Gunpowder did for you.
- What percentage of your target list was penetrated?
- Did you experience a significant/measurable increase in sales?
- What lead you to extend your contract with Gunpowder?

- Has working with Gunpowder in any way caused you to change the way you approach your sales process?
- What were your sales reps saying about their experience with Gunpowder?
- What were your clients saying about their experience with Gunpowder?
- What impressed you most about Gunpowder?
- What was the greatest value you felt Gunpowder delivered
- Would you consider the engagement a success?
- Is there anything you would have changed about the experience?
- Would you recommend Gunpowder to other businesses?

Here's another good case study example, this one created by our client Gatherings Event Planning, which specializes in corporate events.

HENKEL & SCHWARZKOPF CASE STUDY:

A Successful National Sales Meeting

Henkel is the name behind some of North America's best-known brands. From Dial soap to Purex laundry detergent and Got2Be hair styling products, Henkel brands are part of your daily life. While the brands range from detergents to soaps and body washes to advanced engineering adhesives, they all have one thing in common: they make people's lives easier, better, and more beautiful. Henkel has grown rapidly in North America during the past several years and now generates 20% of worldwide sales in this region. Henkel is a global Fortune 500 company headquartered in Germany, and has over 55,000 employees.

"Thanks to Kendra and the Gatherings team for contributing to the success of the Henkel National Sales Meeting. The feedback from attendees was extremely positive, particularly on the downtown location, the hotel facilities, and after meeting activities. Kendra and her team were very attentive to our conference needs." Ian Lum You, Vice President – Sales Henkel Canada

Henkel approached Gatherings Event Planning to organize and manage their national sales meeting. The first step in the process was determining scope, size, and budget. During the initial planning phase, Gatherings engaged in numerous consultations in order to determine the location, style, and objectives of the meeting. Once we determined the location needed to be Toronto, the team from Gatherings started putting together a short list of potential venues. We researched the area and the spaces that would work with Henkel's budget and number of delegates. We presented Henkel with three possible venues and proceeded to do site inspections. Once they decided on the venue—1 King West at King & Yonge, we entered into contract negotiations. This is essential in order to get the best possible price for the client. Typically, the areas that are negotiable are room rates, space rental rates, and food and beverage rates.

Since the company was entertaining delegates from out of town and out of the country, it was important to showcase Toronto. We researched and put forward several ideas for off-site dining experiences and decided on ferry service to the Royal Canadian Yacht Club. We arranged the details, coordinated with the venue on menu and timing, plus secured the ferry service to and from the event. In order to make the trip extra special, we suggested a double decker bus tour of downtown Toronto on the way to the ferry.

Finally, while on site, the Gatherings team set up a hospitality desk in order to answer questions about the area, the meeting agenda, and places to go after being adjourned. We were also on hand for administrative tasks and to keep things running smoothly. This service was well utilized as some delegates needed to fax documents back to their offices in the U.S., host conference calls, and coordinate a management dinner at the last minute. The Gatherings team were able to facilitate all these requests.

Through Gatherings' developed relationships with suppliers and vendors, we were able to secure Henkel discounted rates and special treatment for all their services. We acted as the liaison between the venue, AV company, catering, and the client. We finalized floor plans, production schedules, and daily agendas, and were available throughout the meeting to ensure successful execution.

Event Highlights:

- 3 Day Sales Meeting

- Delegates from United States & Canada

- Venue: 1 King West

- AV Provider: AV Canada

- Off-site dinner at RCYC (Royal Canadian Yacht Club)

- Ferry service to Toronto Island for dinner

- Shuttle service to and from airport

- Accommodations & catering

- Gift bags & welcome packages

USING CASE STUDIES AS MARKETPLACE LEVERAGE

You can use case studies to leverage the brand of your existing customers. You may be working for an unknown company and have only one client, but if that client is a well-known enterprise that you have done good work for, you can leverage their well-known brand onto yours by writing a case study about how your company helped them. This will win visibility and showcase your expertise. Case studies are the great levelers of the business playing field. They can make your company, and you, competitive in a heartbeat.

Here are a few things to keep in mind when developing a case study:

- Prepare a great list of questions to ask your client.
- Get permission to record the interview and have it transcribed.
- Edit the comments you generate during the interview; make sure the client sounds very professional.
- Get permission to use their company name. Anonymous case studies are not nearly as effective as case studies where you cite the real names of people and companies. If the reader can't find the website of the company you worked with, you will lose all of the brand transference.
- If possible, hone in on three industry problems, and show exactly how your company solved those problems.
- Show how you saved money or delivered some kind of measurable return on investment.
- Tell a story with a clear beginning, middle, and end. People love stories, especially stories with major obstacles for the protagonist to overcome. (Avoid jargon and abbreviations; most readers really dislike marketing-speak.)

- Create a compelling title. "ABC Company Case Study" won't cut it.
- Make it pretty. Once you have all the edits finalized and your client has signed off on the piece, give the text to a professional designer who can format it beautifully.

The main reason I like to attach a good case study is that I am usually not in the room with the executive assistant as she runs through the mental list of questions that will determine who gets an appointment (or doesn't) with the boss. Since I'm not there to make my case in person, I like to arm the assistant with as much ammunition as possible, which means offering up as many powerful, relevant reasons why my client is worthy of a slot on the calendar as I can.

"A fact in itself is nothing. It is valuable only for the idea attached to it, or for the proof which it furnishes."
~ CLAUDE BERNARD

A case study is compelling supporting evidence the executive assistant (or anyone else, for that matter) can print off and attach to my letter. I know some people under 20 have a hard time believing that anyone would ever choose to print anything anymore, but suffice to say that this is a generational issue. My advice to you is to learn the average age of your typical client and figure out how someone that age likes to access information. Personally, I think it's always a good idea to make sure your materials print well.

VIDEO ATTACHMENTS

Today's easy-to-access video technology gives you additional ammunition you can use for electronic warfare, as my friend Nancy discovered recently. She called me up for some advice on closing a big deal I had referred to her. I asked her to describe the situation, and what she told me suggested that she was one of two companies in the running for a very big piece of business. She wanted to know whether there was anything she could do to win the business at this late stage of the game.

As it happened, I knew the entrepreneur who was considering using her, let's call him Alex, by means of a mutual acquaintance we'll call Michael. Both gentlemen are under 25 years in age.

I remembered that when I met Michael for the first time, he showed me some of the YouTube clips of his media interviews; he used links to these video clips (which are extremely easy to email) as powerful marketing tools for his business, which was very successful.

It seemed to me that Alex, like his best friend Michael, was an extremely ambitious young man; he was just starting to ramp up his own business. I mentioned to Nancy that speed seemed to be the critical business trait that these two friends had in common: they talk fast, they walk fast, they work fast, and they want their information fast. It seemed obvious that Alex, too, would love YouTube.

I asked Nancy whether she had a happy client who would speak well of her work and let her videotape an interview ASAP. She said she did. I suggested that she record the interview and post it as soon as humanly possible. Emailing a good YouTube link to Alex could nail the account for her and, of course, she could post the clip on her website, as well.

Nancy told me she had plenty of clients that she could record on short notice, but she was curious: why a video clip? Why not have Alex call one of her clients unannounced? (That was one of Nancy's favourite sell-ing strategies, one that had been quite effective for her over the years.) Wouldn't talking directly to a happy client deliver a more authentic mes-sage? Why was it so important to send a YouTube link?

"Maybe I'm being old-fashioned," Nancy said, "and I'm not trying to say that video isn't a great idea...but are you sure this is a deal-maker?"

So I explained: "Nancy, this guy thinks his best friend walks on wa-ter—and Michael uses video clips all the time. I guarantee you that they are emailing video clips back and forth every day. They're young entre-preneurs. This is what young entrepreneurs do. You asked me, and I'm telling you. They don't want to take the time to call someone. They want the information delivered to them. Your YouTube clip is what needs to be authentic. If you want to stand out, today, with this guy...send him a personalized clip."

Nancy sent me her YouTube clip. It was authentic, it delivered real value, and it showcased a history of success with her clients. Perhaps most important of all, it showed that she was willing to work for this man's business. It was delivered in exactly the way her prospect likes to receive information. And it won her the account.

I knew all about the power of video clips from my days at DWL. When I started there, we had very few clients. You might wonder: how on earth did we get Fortune 500 companies to take us seriously when we had so few clients? The answer was simple: the more you know about the people you are prospecting, the more Bulletproofed you will be and the more creative you can be as well.

How did we overcome this obstacle of appearing too small? How did we win instant credibility with a CIO in the first few moments of meet-ing him or her? The answer was simple. At the beginning of the meeting, we played a video clip of the CIO of another client speaking about how we had created a world class intranet for him—on time and under budget.

How do you think the meeting went from there?

After we showed that two minute clip, people wanted to know how we did it. They took us very seriously, because they didn't want to be left behind by their competitors.

My point is that you no longer have to wait for the first meeting to have that kind of impact. Today's video technology allows you to build that kind of competitive advantage into the discussion before you even have a voice-to-voice conversation. Harness the power of that electronic ammunition for your prospecting campaign, especially when you are targeting younger decision makers.

One final piece of advice here: make sure your voice mail message mentions the video link if you do decide to send one. The people you are trying to talk to get lots of emails, and your voice mail message must offer many enticing reasons for them to keep an eye out for and open your message. A video link can and should be one of those enticing reasons.

"Any sufficiently advanced technology is indistinguishable from magic."
~ Arthur C. Clarke

In the next chapter, I'll share some insights on the most exciting and potentially rewarding part of your tactical plan: voice-to-voice combat.

CHAPTER ELEVEN

Tactic 4: Voice-to-voice Combat

"Pressure makes diamonds."
~ GENERAL GEORGE S. PATTON JR.

Congratulations, you've made it to tactic four of the Gunpowder Bulletproof Prospecting System: Voice-to-Voice combat. Here's where all of your research and preparation will pay off. If you've done phases 1, 2, and 3 correctly, these calls won't be cold calls; they'll be **gold calls**.

Are you famished? I hope so, because you have to be if you expect to make good voice-to-voice contact with your target. FAMISHED is an acronym. Here's what it stands for:

F is for Find

Find a point of entry. There are specific people, preferably with signing authority, who can move your sale forward. Find them. Ideally, you should identify more than one person with whom you can speak about your offering.

A is for Ask

Ask permission—"Have I caught you at a good time?" This step is optional. As a medium, the telephone is highly intrusive; there is no point in talking to a person who is not listening to you. By asking when would be a good time to call back, you may be able to get your first commitment. Make a positive impression by respecting the other person's time. If you can tell instantly that the individual you've reached has a positive attitude, you can skip this step.

M is for Match

Match the person's tonality and pace of speaking. This is very important. You must establish conversational harmony. Let the other person's tone and pacing serve as the ground rules for this conversation.

I is for Intention

State your intention with confidence. Say exactly why you are calling: "I'm calling to set up a meeting with your CIO."

142

S is for Success story

Share a success story to establish your credibility. Start by identifying the people and/or companies your company has worked with. Briefly and authoritatively tell the story of why they chose you and why they decided to stay with you. To gain credibility, you must share success stories that highlight benefits of interest to the person you are talking to.

H is for Hot buttons

Address your target's hot buttons. These are the specific benefits you identified in your research, and used in both your voice mail message and your follow-up email. Review these briefly here.

E is for Expect the No

Expect the "No". People are busy. Don't imagine they will instantly buy into your message. Anticipate resistance; don't be thrown by it. Get ready for it by remembering the power of three: have at least three questions ready when you hear the "No," and be ready with a rebuttal. This is an extremely important bulletproofing step. We call this voice-to-voice combat for a reason; be prepared.

D is for Do it again

Do it again. Make at least three direct, polite requests for the face-to-face meeting. Give different reasons for each. If you only make one attempt to get the meeting, you are not hungry enough!

You must be FAMISHED if you expect to win the meeting. And yes, that's both an acronym and a state of mind. **The most important thing to do as you implement this is have fun with people!**

Closely study the sequence of objectives I shared with you, because they incorporate many years of personal experience in both setting appointments with C-level contacts (and other important decision makers, such as founders and sole proprietors) and training others to set those appointments.

I now make a point of telling CEOs that each and every member of their sales team must absolutely, positively be FAMISHED before they are sent out into the marketplace. Of course, I don't mean that salespeople must be literally hungry (although who knows, that may help). I mean that they must be willing to become completely prepared—Bulletproofed—before they start improvising phone conversations with the most important people in the buying organization. What's more, they must be confident. A big part of that confidence must come from role-playing with a colleague or sales manager. Reading this book is not enough; you must actually practice what's in this book!

CEOs take note: practice and role-playing are absolutely essential before you allow someone to represent your brand.

"Take advantage of every opportunity to practice your communication skills so that when important occasions arise, you will have the gift, the style, the sharpness, the clarity, and the emotions to affect other people."
~JIM ROHN

THE HEART OF THE SYSTEM

What you are really looking at when you look at the simple word FAMISHED is the heart of the Gunpowder Bulletproof Prospecting System. With that in mind, let's look at each of these critical elements in more depth.

Find a Point of Entry

Many salespeople call the same single contact over and over again, with no backup plan to guide them if that person doesn't respond or turns out to be the wrong person. There are some situations where calling a single individual is appropriate, of course—namely, an opportunity where you know for sure that the one person you're trying to reach is the only individual in the entire buying organization who can help you move forward in the sale. These situations, though, are relatively rare. Most of the time, you will want to have more than one person targeted within a large organization.

It's quite common for sales managers to buy a database, download a pile of information that connects to a specific territory, and then email the data to the relevant sales team member. Both the manager and salesperson simply sleepwalk through the data that's been extracted—regardless of how out of date or incomplete it may be, or how many people in the enterprise it overlooks.

One data source is not enough! In most cases, you must have *multiple* possible points of entry to call if you hope to find a single viable point of entry.

If you only have one person to call, you are not ready to reach out for voice-to-voice contact. Do some research, either online or by calling ahead to ask who the key players are. (Refer to Chapter 6 for information on target list generation.) Remember, to be successful you must work from abundance, don't limit yourself with only one contact person.

Questions to ask yourself while you are looking for likely points of entry include:

- Is this really the best point of entry for me to sell to this organization? How do I know?
- Who does this person report to?

- Does this person's role or title remind me of the role or title of another decision maker my organization has sold to?

- Have I confirmed the information I now have by consulting more than one source? How sure am I that the names and titles I have are really up to date?

- Does the person I am trying to reach out to have an assistant? (If so, I automatically know that I have at least one more possible point of entry to the account.)

- Do I know the names of at least three people I could call within this account?

Key point: if you start your discussions with the executive assistant who works for the president or founder, you can save yourself weeks or months of wondering (and guessing) who you should be talking to. I can honestly tell you when I was a new salesperson I learned this important step the hard way. I spent months flying around the country meeting with people who I thought had decision-making authority only to find myself in the run around. Take the extra **few moments to verify that your decision maker** really is the key to unlocking this great account. Don't be fooled, sometimes people give you the wrong information because they don't know and they guess. Find another senior source within the target to confirm your information. This step will save you time and money. Remember, in Fortune 1000 accounts there is always more than one decision maker. Often we sell our clients into one division and once we have success there, we spread through the entire organization with a lot more ease.

ASK PERMISSION (OPTIONAL)

This step, as I have said, is a judgment call. After briefly identifying yourself, you will either:

a) ask permission, or

b) not ask permission

Asking for permission sounds like this: "Ms. Smith, have I caught you at a good time?"

You will only ask permission if the first few syllables you hear from the other person suggest that he or she is harried, frustrated, or distracted. In essence, what you're doing here is proving that you are flexible enough to offer to reschedule the call.

If you have any doubt in your mind that the person has responded positively and optimistically to your first few words, ask permission, and then try to find out if there's a better time for you to call. Be ready to fast-forward to the point where you share the reason for your call. That's what people want to know: why are you calling?

Very often, the sequence will sound like this:

Target: "What is it? What do you want?"

You: "Have I caught you at a good time?"

Target: "No. I'm getting ready for a meeting."

You: "What would be a better time for me to call back?"

Target: "Um...anytime tomorrow before eleven. (Or: "Well, what's this about, anyway?" When you hear this, give the person a *brief* preview of one of your benefit statements, then, get ready for the "no" have a question ready.)

When people are busy, we must prove to them very quickly why it makes sense for them to keep listening to us. How much attention do you pay when you are busy and someone calls you to talk about something he or she thinks you should buy? How many seconds does it take for you to disengage from that conversation? For me, it's less than two. Don't sell—add value!

This second step illustrates how important it is to be able to make good decisions very quickly during your calls. You must decide almost instantaneously whether or not there is enough rapport in your initial exchanges and enough positive energy in the other person's voice for you to begin the conversation in earnest. The first few seconds of a call is your opportunity to win a friend. How can you add value? The hardest part of this work is getting your decision maker live on the phone. Practice the tough situations, use humour if it's appropriate. Adding a smile to someone's day is no small feat, and it will be remembered.

MATCH THE OTHER PERSON'S TONALITY AND PACE OF SPEAKING

This step happens more or less simultaneously with the next step, stating your intention, but it's so important that it is worthy of practice and study on its own.

Most salespeople plunge right into the opening of the conversation without bothering to think about tonality or pace at all, and then they wonder why they're not getting anywhere on the phone. If you listen very carefully, you will notice within a few seconds whether the person you are talking to is speaking quickly, slowly, or somewhere in between. You will also notice whether the tone is low, high, or moderate. You must make a decision about how best to match both tonality and pace, based on only the first few sentences you hear.

I can tell when one of my own salespeople is ignoring this step. The pacing and tonality of their side of the call never changes, even after they've made dozens of calls on a given day. That relentless sameness in the calling pattern means the salesperson either isn't listening for the conversational tone and pace of the other person, or isn't trying to match what he or she is hearing.

My husband and daughter will tease me sometimes when I start speaking to people in their accents. They'll say to me right after I have hung up the phone, "Why are you talking with an English accent?" The answer, of course, is that I was just speaking to a person in England! **Good salespeople are conversational chameleons.** When hiring salespeople, I am always on the lookout for people who can make these kinds of transitions easily. To some people it comes very natural while others have to pay attention to the person they are speaking with. Which type of person are you?

INTENTION

We're already on the fourth step of the call, but notice that it should only have taken us a few seconds to get here.

People need to know the reason for your call, so tell them: "The reason I am calling you is to book a meeting with Mr. Jones." Or: "My intention is to set up a meeting between the two of us for sometime next week."

You must say exactly why you are calling. You must be clear and unambiguous about your intentions. And you must sound absolutely confident as you tell the other person what you want as an end result from this conversation. All of this is non-negotiable. None of what follows will work if you are not absolutely transparent about your intentions during the call. If you are not transparent, people will instantly disengage. They will completely tune out of whatever you are trying to say, because they will be trying to figure out exactly what it is that you are after.

Key point: nobody likes to be sold to. You are not selling; you have genuine value you want to add to this person's operation, and you are always willing to discuss that value in an open and direct way. Never forget that!

"Price is what you pay. Value is what you get."
~WARREN BUFFETT

If you don't say exactly why you are calling, you will not be perceived as being up-front, which means you will be perceived as a stereotypical tricky salesperson. People want to hang up when they can tell you are not being straight with them. Is that the response you want to elicit? If you get nothing else from this book, get this: doing what most salespeople do will get you the results most salespeople get.

SUCCESS STORIES FOR CREDIBILITY

How do you establish trust with people you don't know?

When prospecting for new customers you have 30 seconds to get someone's attention, prove your worthiness and establish a memorable experience. You are tested and judged in 30 second sound bites in many areas of selling.

Establishing and keeping a high degree of trust with your prospects throughout the entire sales cycle can significantly speed up the process of closing new business. One of the most powerful ways of establishing trust is through testimonials, case studies -- the good work you do for others.

This is where all the research, practice, and role-playing you did before the call begin to pay off. You must know exactly which stories you will be telling during this call, and you must be particularly clear about the very first story you intend to tell. If you do not know which story you plan to tell this person, and why, you are not ready to make the call.

Without credibility, there is no reason for the other person to agree to meet with you, or even to continue the conversation. During the call, you will find that the "S" of success stories inevitably overlaps with the "H" of hot buttons. I have suggested that you focus on the stories first because doing so forces you to identify the specific companies and individuals you will need to reference in order to get the other person to take the call, and you, seriously enough to put everything else aside for a moment.

The anatomy: A recognizable client name; clearly state the problem they had and how you solved their problem. You have ten seconds!

An example:

> "Our client Corporate Express came to us because they wanted help setting meetings with key decision makers. We worked with them for seven years straight booking those important meetings and at the end of that time they had won 90% of the Fortune 1000 companies. This made them a very attractive target for Staples who acquired them in 2008."

> "I had an opportunity to give a keynote talk to a group of students at Harvard Business School last June. One of the students named Ivan came up to thank me because he was afraid to do any type of cold call and my talk had inspired him. Two months later he called me to say he loved prospecting in his new job because he never had to do a cold call again. He had learned how to turn cold prospects into warm ones following our Gunpowder bulletproof process."

HOT BUTTONS

Of course, the success stories you tell during this call must connect to the actual value you have delivered to real companies. What you think, believe, or imagine you can do for your decision maker may be interesting to you, but it will not be as interesting to the other person...unless you can back it up with the names and addresses of real people at real companies who are happy they worked with you.

If you don't have at least one real case study you can point to, complete with real contacts who will vouch for the merits of your product or service, *you are not ready to make this call.*

EXPECT A "NO"

This is where we can quickly separate the amateurs from the professionals. Amateurs lose energy, optimism, and traction on the call when they encounter the inevitable obstacles that accompany any form of telephone prospecting. Professionals know that the people they will be reaching out to are going to push back, they expect them to push back, and do not become exhausted, deflated, or desperate when they hear some variation of the word "No."

I try to work closely with any salesperson who is hesitant about making at least three attempts to respond in a confident, compelling way to the "No" that always arises during prospecting. If I happen to hear a salesperson give up on the call and hang up without making this kind of effort, I will be the one who pushes back. I'll say, "Bill, I didn't hear any voice-to-voice combat on that call!"

Voice-to-voice combat means confident, poised responses to the "No" we know is coming. Voice-to-voice combat is where salespeople earn their pay. It may feel awkward at first, but this is definitely a skill that can be learned. Once you learn it, you will have earned a spot in the top tier of salespeople.

The key to voice-to-voice combat is having good questions ready. If you can uncover the real reason someone does not want to meet with you, you have a chance to come back to them with a success story that ties into and overcomes their objection.

Too many salespeople tell me that they ask questions in order to "maintain control of the conversation" or "keep the flow going." I suppose there is something to be said for these goals, but the reason I ask questions is that very often people will not understand why I am actually calling. Why would I conceal that? My questions support my intent, and they are big part of my job. That job is to find a way to effectively educate people about how I am going to help them. I can't possibly do that if I don't ask good questions!

"Successful people ask better questions, and as a result, they get better answers."
~ TONY ROBBINS

DO IT AGAIN

The last step is here to make sure that you remind yourself that there really is a way forward for the vast majority of the people with whom you will be speaking. Your job is to find that way forward—persistently, pragmatically, and with a sense of certainty. That's the reason we do it again, as necessary. We believe the potential for value is still there.

This do-it-again principle plays out in three different time frames:

- During the initial voice-to-voice exchange.
- After you've received the first clear "Yes" or "No" from the decision maker.
- In your long-term follow-up campaign, where you believe that there's a good potential match but the other person is still unwilling to commit to a meeting.

Let's look at each of these three time frames in turn, and see how the do-it-again principle applies in each scenario.

During the first voice-to-voice contact

It should become second nature for you to make three purposeful, direct, and confident attempts to secure the face-to-face meeting. Your aim should be to wrestle your way onto this person's calendar. Remember to think of yourself as a Navy SEAL. Navy SEALs aren't impatient, stressed, or easily spooked by obstacles; they're totally focused on the mission, and they're models of discipline and purpose—even when they have to revise their plans on the ground.

After you receive the first clear "Yes" or "No" from the decision maker

If it's a "Yes, we'd be interested in talking about this," then press forward and try to book the appointment. (Don't give a sales presentation on the phone.) If it's a "No," you must find out why the person is saying "No." Recently, one of my own salespeople got a "No" which was based in this explanation from the decision maker: "We're already doing that." This answer deflated her a little, but she gathered as much information as she could, ended the call, and eventually shared her experience on the call with the rest of us during a team meeting. After about 10 minutes, we were able to determine that what her prospect was using really wasn't at all what she was proposing; it was something entirely different. She called again the next day, more confident than ever about the value of her solution—and booked the meeting.

When you hear "Call us in a few weeks/months/quarters."

Sometimes you'll have a good conversation with a decision maker that, for whatever reason, concludes with the decision that it makes the most sense to continue the discussion at a later point in time. I have two rules of thumb that I like to follow in this situation. First and foremost, I ask why. If the decision maker tells me to call back in three months, I'm curious about what made the person suggest that particular time frame for our next call. Is something special happening between now and then? If so, what is it? And second, I want to know what this person's timeline is, so can cut it in half. In other words, if the person tells me to call back in three months, I want to call back in 45 days. The prospect should know that I'm still interested and that I'm taking responsibility for what happens next in the relationship. Cutting the time frame for the next "check-in" is a great way to do this, and it has the added advantage of accelerating the sales cycle.

BUT WHERE'S THE SCRIPT?

As you may have noticed, I've shared the basic principles behind this all-important series of calls with you before sharing the calling script.

Some salespeople think that the calling script is the center of any prospecting campaign. Actually, the principles are much, much more important than the script. The script may get you through one call, but your job is to determine whether there really is a potential match for what you offer, and that is likely to take more than one discussion with more than one person. If you only have one script, you can only have one conversation, and fighting your way onto the person's calendar is likely to take more than one session of voice-to-voice combat. **And remember, you must sound knowledgeable not scripted**

"Ambition is the path to success; persistence is the vehicle you arrive in."
~ WILLIAM EARDLEY, IV

Once you understand this, you are in a position to use a calling script as a rough model for the multiple calls you are likely to place in your quest to figure out whether there's a potential match. Here's a possible example.

Hi (Executive assistant to the CEO),

I'm (Name). I work for to the COO of SoftSpin Data, and I need your guidance in arranging a meeting with one of the people at your company. Do you have a moment?

We have an application for your website that eliminates 84% of email inquiries and call-center inquiries.

For example, when your customers or employees visit your website and get frustrated because they can't find what they're looking for quickly enough, this almost always results in an escalation to your help desk.

SoftSpin uses an Advanced Language Recognition Technology, which allows a user to search your website using natural language dialogue. They're able to find the information they are seeking faster and more efficiently, even if their search includes grammatical errors and spelling mistakes.

This can ultimately garner hundreds of thousands of dollars in savings.

I've been asked by the COO of my company to set up a meeting with the right person at your company.

Who would you recommend as the most senior executive who would be interested in this kind of process redesign?

Assuming that she says something that is meant to connect you to a manager, procurement, or some other non-C-level contact:

(Shirley), I appreciate your help. Is (John) at a level within the organization that would actually implement process redesign? As you know, to save so much money it usually takes a senior strategic visionary to actually implement large cost savings. We will be happy to speak to management level after we have confirmed at a senior level that this is a strategic direction our two companies will head in.

Notice that we had a question ready: Is (John) at a level within the organization that would actually implement process redesign?

Other possible questions include:

- How long is the current average wait time for customers to reach a live person on your help desk?
- What are you doing right now to make it easy for customers to find what they're looking for on your website?
- How much are you currently spending to resolve questions that people could answer for themselves if they could navigate your website more efficiently?

Here's another example:

Good morning/afternoon_____, this is David Butler at Bridge Group. I am hoping you can help direct me. Do you have a moment?

We provide our customers with team and project communications tools on capital projects around the world. For example, Fluor, one of the world's largest engineering, procurement, and construction companies, has deployed our best practices on over 100 plus projects in 25 countries around the world.

Who would be responsible for project execution of large capital projects at your company?

The primary markets we service are the Engineering, Oil & Gas, Infrastructure, and Power and Utilities marketplaces. Some of our clients—like BigCo, the world's second largest energy company—have put the benefits of our experience to work on a global level.

I have been asked to set up an educational session with your senior management. I would like to know who at your company would be interested in learning about global best practices and compliance for capital project execution on large construction projects.

I know project collaboration is one of the most important issues your company is facing, and we would like to make sure the right members of your team are included in this educational session.

Notice that we had a question ready: Who would be responsible for project execution of large capital projects at your company?

Other possible questions include:

- Do you have a project execution team?
- Who is in charge of building the facilities?
- Some of the people we have worked with in the past have had titles like CEO, Senior Manager of Project Controls, and Vice President of Engineering; who do you think we should be reaching out to?

Think of yourself as the Navy SEAL whose job it is to engage in maneuvers that will win you a spot on the calendar—a spot that can be held and defended. The advice I've given you thus far in this chapter will get you through your mission successfully. If you are committed to the driving purpose of your mission, you will succeed.

"When I chased after money, I never had enough. When I got my life on purpose and focused on giving of myself and everything that arrived into my life, then I was prosperous."
~WAYNE DYER

Notice that a tactical plan is different from a set of instructions. A tactical plan is a flexible, objective-driven map of options that allows you to make the best choices—often the best life-or-death choices—in support of your mission. Instructions are something you follow without thinking, when you imagine someone else is responsible for your success or failure. As any good Navy SEAL can attest, the person who is responsible for getting you to a defensible position is you.

Your primary goal is to initiate voice-to-voice contact and use the FAMISHED model to find out whether there's a potential match with what you offer. If you determine, beyond a shadow of a doubt, that there really is no such match, you will close the lead and move on. If you determine that there is a match, however, your secondary mission is to schedule a face-to-face meeting so you can make your case in person. You and you alone, will determine the success or failure of that mission.

Now that you know the tactical plan and have studied it carefully, don't get too distracted with the "how." Focus on the mission objectives.

Remember where you are going and why.

OUR FAVOURITE RESPONSES TO COMMON OBJECTIONS

As we've discussed, objections are inevitable. You must expect them and be prepared to rebut them. Here's a summary of the most common objections our people hear during voice-to-voice combat and the kinds of responses we've found to be most useful in turning those objections around. Take these 10 common objections and make your own responses and include mini testimonials whenever you can. The more lucid your response, the more effective you will be, so practice, practice, practice until you can handle all 10 creatively and with confidence and enthusiasm. Then print these pages and post it in your calling area, where you can consult them often.

Objection: We already have a provider/contract; it goes for another (x) years.
- Are you currently satisfied with your provider?
- I'd like to introduce our differences and capabilities so that when the time to review does come up you are familiar with our company.
- We don't intend to infringe on your current contracts, but we are hoping to provide you with a cost and service comparison. You may find that savings are available with a higher service level if you partner with us.

Objection: We just signed a new contract last month
- I'm curious: did you include our company in the RFP (Request for Proposal) process?
  - (Yes.) Do you mind if I ask who you went with? How long will the contract be in place? (Check back in six months to see if the person/organization is still satisfied)

- (No.) Well, I can understand that you wouldn't want to go through the whole process again, but my VP would appreciate some of your time to introduce our differences and capabilities in the near future, regardless of your current obligations.

Objection: We have taken the RFP process too far at this point. We are down to two or three vendors now and will not consider any more.

- Did you consider our company prior to this selection?
  - (Yes.) Can I ask where we went off track? (The person will usually tell you why you weren't selected/were not a good fit.)
  - (No.) Do you mind if I send an email with further information? You could also take a moment to check our website; you may be surprised by the differences we offer. We are the leader in this area and work with A, B, C, and D companies. One hour with us: will save you..., will expand your understanding..., will teach you..., will show you why we are the leader in this area. Would you consider a brief conference call with my VP? He has valuable information on our best practices and methodologies that you may not be aware of. One hour with us could save you a great deal of frustration. (Be sure to fill in the dots above and below with the big benefits that apply to your product or service.)

Objection: We had a contract with your company before and we weren't satisfied (bad experience)

- I'm sorry to hear that. How long ago was that?
- We have upgraded our services in many ways, and I am not familiar with your company and would appreciate introducing

myself and our new capabilities.

- (If they tell you specifics on the problems) We have definitely taken steps to ensure these situations no longer come up. Could you take a few moments with my VP? He'd be happy to address your prior dissatisfaction and see if there is any way to rectify the situation.

- Your business means a great deal to us, and the reason for my call is to set up a meeting with you and our SVP. She wants to personally apologize for the bad experience your company had and find ways we could compensate you for our short comings. In addition she would like to bring you up to speed with the changes we have implemented to ensure our service levels are world class.

Objection: This is not a priority for us right now/not on our radar this quarter.

- I can understand that you're busy with other things. I have information on our best practices and methodologies that you may not have considered. If I could present cost savings over your present provider, wouldn't that make it a priority for this quarter?

Objection: We have a long-standing relationship with our current provider/happy with what we've got in place/not looking to change.

- May I ask who you're with? I understand that if you're happy it can be a trial to change providers, but I have information on our best practices and methodologies that you may not have considered. We are the leader in this area for these reasons... Companies like A,B,C, and D do business with us because we were able to show...

- When was the last time you went into the market to educate yourself on the best practices in today's busy economy?

- I'd like to present a comparison on pricing that may demonstrate a significant cost savings over your current provider because of...

Objection: Our current provider is related to the CEO/founder/whoever.

- It's understandable that you have to go with what the boss says, but if you could present better service and cost savings to the CEO, would that perhaps make him reconsider? We can walk you through a step-by-step comparison that can arm you with the information you need to move your company ahead of your competition.

Objection: I don't have time to discuss this right now.

- What would be a better time to call back?
- May I send an email with further information that you can peruse at your leisure?

Objection: I don't think your product would be a good match with our current systems/needs.

- Check to see if what you're offering qualifies. If it does, then ask good questions that lead to your product offering.
- We'd like to update you on our recent advances with our offerings. If you just take a short time for a conference call, I think you will find we have some valuable information on current market trends and ways to improve productivity/cut costs. (Obviously, this one depends on the product offering.)

Objection: I don't take calls from vendors. (Or: prospect sends you to a recorded – "How to Become a Vendor with our Company" message.)

- Go ahead and leave your best compelling message and then try to find a new contact.

- If this pushback is from an executive assistant, try to find direct line and/or email to the main decision maker.

Objection: I don't believe anyone can beat the pricing I am getting right now.

- We are very interested in providing a cost comparison, but we also want to take just a few moments on a conference call to let you know our best practices and methodologies, because they offer excellent service standards and insights into managing your programs in a more effective manner.

Objection: I worked for your company before and I know all about your offering already.

- Wow, that's great. How long ago?
- We'd love the opportunity to update you on our recent changes, product offerings, etc.

Objection: I'm well versed in this industry and don't need any more information.

- Will you be reviewing your programs this year?
- When is a good time to check back?
- May I ask who you are currently working with?
- Did you know we are the number one choice in your industry? (back it up with your case studies)
- Why did you choose to work with this company?

Objection: You would have to talk to Joe and he is in a meeting/booked solid for the next month.

- Find a good time to call back, even if it's weeks from now.
- Send a great email.
- Try to reach Joe very early or late in the day, or over the lunch hour

to see if you can catch him between meetings.

- Be persistent!

Objection: We don't talk to any vendors until the RFP process is coming up. We will contact you if we are interested in including you.

- We respect the RFP process and many of our clients appreciated
  learning about our expertise before finalizing their RFP. Would you
  like to know why? Our methodologies helped them to shape a better document. They were able to really compare apples to apples. In
  fact, our documentation could save you many hours of hard work.
  There are some very big reasons we are the leader in this industry.
  (use this provided you are prepared to help them write the RFP
  and you can document your leadership in the marketplace. If you
  can't, you might say "We are the fastest growing...because of ...")

- Try to find out when the contract ends.

- Try a contact either higher up or in an appropriate area to the
  product offering who may be more open to talking to you.

TIMING YOUR CALLS

Don't expect people to call you back. They are too busy, and senior
people are in meetings all day. You must expect people not to be at their
desk the first time you call and not to return your calls. "I left a message"
is not an acceptable strategy. To get your target contact live on the phone,
you must be prepared to:

- Call early.
- Call at lunch.
- Call right before 5:00 PM

- Call at 5:00 PM
- Call after 5:00 PM

If you can be certain that your number is blocked from the receiving phone's view, you can call as many times as you want to try to reach someone voice-to-voice and then abandon the call without looking like a stalker. (This "call blocking" is an essential piece of battlefield technology, if you ask me.)

FINAL THOUGHTS ON VOICE-TO-VOICE COMBAT

Voice-to-voice combat is the art of wrestling your way onto the target's calendar. It's non-negotiable—it's the pivot-point of your whole campaign. It's what this entire book has been pointing you toward. If you execute this part of the campaign successfully, you're in the game, and probably on the inside track. If you don't execute this part successfully, you're not in the game. It's as simple as that.

In all probability, you won't execute the principles of successful voice-to-voice combat perfectly the first time you attempt it. It takes practice. If you worked for me, I would insist that you engage in several hours of role-play with me, a senior colleague, or your own manager before trying it live with a client. Then, when you went live, I would insist that you debrief and role-play extensively immediately following the first voice-to-voice exchange that didn't go well. (That's a very likely early outcome, by the way.)

If you get slaughtered during one of these early calls—and you probably will—you will face a fateful choice. You can do one of three things:

- Figure out exactly what went wrong and find a way to do it better on your next call.

- Try to fake your way through the next call without quite knowing what tripped you up last time.
- Give up and go back to calling mid-level contacts.
- Only the first option leads to sustainable high-level performance.

Remember: there can be no script for this kind of exchange, so don't try to memorize one. Your mental preparation for voice-to-voice combat is far more important than any advance memorization. There is a reason that people and nations go into battle: they are driven by a sense of Purpose, with a capital P. There must be a similarly inspiring, indomitable reason for you to reach out to people who can benefit from what you offer; your own Purpose with a capital P. Think back to Chapter 2 when you first considered what your motivation is. Once that larger sense of Purpose drives your intent during these calls, you will have all the scripting you need.

Congratulations! You've reached the end of the Gunpowder Bulletproof Prospecting System. Armed with these tools, you are well on your way to blasting open some big doors. The next chapter offers one final tool, but it's only used in extreme cases, so it's not included as one of the four key tactics.

CHAPTER TWELVE

For Emergency Use Only

"Success is how high you bounce when you hit bottom."
~ GENERAL GEORGE S. PATTON JR.

Although the Gunpowder Bulletproof Prospecting System provides you with the tools to launch a successful campaign, you will still, on occasion, encounter strong resistance. But even when you encounter extremely stiff resistance—the kind that causes your competitors to abandon the very idea of staking out a defensible position—you can still lead the prospecting campaign. I'll show you how in this chapter.

There's a variation to the four-tactic system I've shared with you in this book. One that's designed for especially challenging situations; situations where the prospective buyer, for whatever reason, has a strong predisposition against buying (or even discussing) the product or service you represent. This is nothing less than a sales emergency, and I call the variation that is designed to address it "bombing the beach." The example below demonstrates how to use this variation.

---

*"If you can find a path with no obstacles,
it probably doesn't lead anywhere."*
~ FRANK A. CLARK

BOMBING THE BEACH

The new client I had just taken on had what seemed to be a perfect business model. Corporations who had miscalculated and overpaid their taxes to the government could get most of that money back, with no up-front investment to secure our client's services. Period.

Let me repeat that. There was no downside, as in literally not one penny down...and the potential upside was staggering. Hundreds of thousands, perhaps even millions of dollars in overpaid taxes were returned to corporations. My client took a commission on the amount of overpaid taxes recovered from the government. The corporations got to add massive amounts of found money directly to their bottom line.

I thought, "Who wouldn't want to talk about that?"

It seemed like the easiest assignment we had gotten in a very, very long time. Our new client had been in business for over 20 years. They had collected hundreds of client testimonials from banks, large blue chip companies, and average midsized businesses. They had a history of great success. We had wonderful testimonials to work with, and we had some great benefit points to discuss in our voice mail messages. We created some compelling email messages, and started making calls. And we got slaughtered on the beach.

Everybody hung up on us. I put some of my very best people on this account, and they got absolutely butchered whenever they made voice-to-voice contact. I don't mean they dealt with skeptical prospects. I mean they dealt with people who hung up on them the minute they figured out what the call was about! I decided I should try making some calls myself. And I got hung up on the minute I told people what the call was about!

What I finally realized was that my client was suffering from what other people in the industry were doing. Virtually anyone with a Certified Accountant designation could put up a shingle and offer this service, and lots of people were. The CFOs we were targeting were getting hundreds of calls every week. In addition, some of the people who were competing with my client weren't doing a very good job, and were leaving their clients unhappy.

All of this created a bad perception of the industry as a whole. As a result, there was just too much initial resistance. We couldn't get a foothold. We had to come up with a way to get us past that initial resistance. We stopped the campaign. I called my client, told him about our experience and asked him for more time to prepare an assault.

Then I called my old sales manager from Peak Performance Training Company, Gregory Cleary. Gregory was now running his own sales coaching business in the U.S., Active Coaching. I told him my story and told him that I had never experienced such a hostile reaction in all my days of selling. Gregory shared his approach for dealing with stiff resistance, and I was certainly glad that he did, because it worked like a charm.

Here's what we did:

Gregory started out by telling me, in essence, that I needed more ammunition to soften up the beach before our people stormed ashore. There were five components to the ammunition we created for this situation.

- We designed a memorable, professionally produced postcard with a visual tie-in to something that could be eaten. (In our case, it was a tin of mints. This allowed us to play off the value message: "Your business means a mint to us.")
- We put one of our client testimonials on the back of that postcard. (We could also recover a "mint" in overpaid taxes, at no risk to the client!)
- We included our contact information on the back of the postcard. (Nobody called us back, but that's beside the point. Our goal was to create awareness and make a future relationship possible, and including our contact information was an important part of that.)
- We put the completed postcard into a bubble envelope with a nice tin of mints, and sent them to the people we wanted to turn into prospects. (The total cost per gift package ended up being under $2.50. I would not spend more.)

- We repeated the process over a period of three days, sending different postcard messages and different edible items every day, for a total of three different mailings; each creative, memorable, and delicious. (My favourite was the one where we sent a Hundred Grand candy bar to back up a testimonial about recovering over $100,000 for a bank.)

Then we started making the calls.

After sending out the "bombs" we had designed, our Sales Development Manager went from scheduling zero meetings a week to scheduling five meetings a week!

You can easily adapt this system to the situations where your own targets are putting up unexpectedly stiff resistance. Just remember that, unlike just about every other tactic I've shared with you in this book, this one does have a cost issue that must be managed carefully. You do want to leave a powerful, memorable sensory impression, but you don't want to (or have to) go overboard on the pieces you send. With a very modest investment, we were able to get people to respond positively to our client's name on the very first call following the mailings. By the way, many people reported that the goodies we had passed along had become coveted treats around the office.

Remember that there's always a way to win...even when you encounter resistance!

"Winning isn't everything, but wanting to win is."
~VINCE LOMBARDI.

CHAPTER THIRTEEN

Lead The Assault

*"We herd sheep, we drive cattle, we lead people.
Lead me, follow me, or get out of my way."*
~ GENERAL GEORGE S. PATTON JR.

This book is about leadership in prospecting and, by extension, about leadership in the world of business. I believe that the single most important thing to understand about any aspect of leadership in business is accountability.

In order for the system I have shared with you to work, you must assume full accountability for implementing each tactic of the Gunpowder Bulletproof Prospecting System (the Intelligence Briefing and Reconnaissance, First Contact, Electronic Warfare, and Voice-to-Voice Combat). That means being accountable for Bulletproofing yourself by:

- Doing the necessary upfront research with insiders, stakeholders, competitors, clients, and front liners.
- Identifying your value proposition.
- Building and revising your target acquisition list.
- Updating your Hot Pad (the top 20 targets on your list).
- Creating the right relationships with gatekeepers and executive assistants.
- Maintaining tenacity and forward momentum on the call. Be creative.
- Calling repeatedly, from a position of abundance, until you reach the right players (either a C-level decision maker or that person's executive assistant).
- Maintaining the mindset necessary to engage positively and optimistically with everyone in the organization.
- Engaging in voice-to-voice combat until you wrestle your way onto the decision maker's calendar. Be prepared for the no and turn it into a YES!

Personal accountability is the engine which drives the entire sales process, not just the prospecting phase—and it is absolutely essential for anyone who intends to implement this program and prospect effectively at the top level of any enterprise.

Once you cultivate sufficient personal accountability to prospect in the way I have taught you to in this book, I believe you will be able to handle virtually anything that comes up later on in the sales process. After you schedule the initial meeting and start making your case, personal accountability is what will enable you to lead the discussion, evaluate the alternatives, and close the deal.

"You already have every characteristic necessary for success... if you recognize, claim, develop and use them all."
~ ZIG ZIGLAR

A former client of mine once shared a story in our local paper on a topic near and dear to the hearts of all salespeople: Those Lying Clients. The story went like this, more or less. A certain contact agreed to meet with my client and then got cold feet when it came time to make a decision and launch the program. Now, this process repeated itself not once or twice, but five times.

Then my client agreed to meet with the same contact at the same company for a sixth time. My client had received a call from this person, who asked for help in creating a proposal for a new project. During the meeting, the following dialogue took place.

My Client: "It's nice to talk to you, but we're a little skeptical about putting another proposal together around this."
Prospect: "No, no—don't be skeptical. We really do need this."

My Client: "Okay. Have you got a budget for this?"

Prospect: "Yes."

My Client: "Really? There are actual dollars put aside for this?"

Prospect: "Absolutely."

My Client: "You're certain?"

Prospect: "Positive."

My Client: "And you, personally, can make the decision? You won't have to go to your boss?"

Prospect: "No, there's no need to get an okay from anyone else. This project is entirely my call."

So my client spent 15 hours creating the proposal for the project. A week later, he got together with his contact and asked, "Are we good to go?"

The contact shook his head and said, "Well, not quite. It turns out I need to go to the CEO for budget approval."

The deal died.

Now, the lesson my client drew from this experience was twofold. First, clients always lie. Do clients ALWAYS lie? Maybe "sometimes "And second, it makes more sense to begin prospecting at the top of the organization than it does to prospect anywhere else. I certainly agree with that second point, but I think there's a larger lesson lurking in the middle of this story, a lesson about accountability.

Personally, I don't believe this customer was lying about budget when my client asked whether he could make the decision independently. It seems more likely to me that he had some qualms about what my client was offering, and was uncomfortable doing business with him. I think the big loss here was not uncovering the real reason why.

You may well be sitting with the decision maker, but if you have left some gaping piece of doubt, that decision maker will never sign off with you, and will inevitably deflect to a higher authority. Case in point: I have a girlfriend named Diana Black. She told me a story years ago about how she named her company Tippin and Black Resources Ltd. solely for the purpose of deflection. If you were a salesperson and Diana didn't like what you'd come up with, she'd look you in the eye and say "I will have to think about it and ask my partner, Tippin (I think Tippin was her maiden name).

Many people just don't like delivering bad news. There is only one way out of this trap, and it's the same way out of all the various traps that present themselves as you are prospecting: personal accountability. That's what leads to good questions and second chances. That's what leads to getting it right when something is wrong.

Assuming that, for whatever reason, I found myself dealing with the same decision maker about the same proposal, this is how I would handled the situation:

Prospect: "It turns out I need to go to the CEO for budget approval."
Me: "I think I have missed something along the way. I know that earlier you said you had the budget, and now I think you're being polite because I've let you down in some way. You don't really want to do business with me. I can understand if you don't like my proposal, but I want to learn for the next time. Where did I fall down?"

Now, this situation may have arisen because I failed to Bulletproof myself properly by having all of the decision makers present. However, if the reason my prospect was kicking it upstairs was because of something I missed in creating the proposal, isn't it better to "throw myself on the sword" in a polite way, by assuming full accountability for any problem that may have arisen? Won't I learn more that way, rather than by running an internal monologue about how this prospect just lied to me? Or, even worse, about how all prospects lie to me?

The example I've just shared with you didn't arise during the prospecting phase, of course—but I think the accountability principle applies throughout the sales cycle. We are always selling something. Early on in the process, we are selling the right to be heard and the right to schedule a face-to-face meeting with the target contact. Later on, we are selling the idea of consummating a business relationship together. Regardless of where we are in the process, we will get further faster by leading the process. And the best way to lead the process is to assume full accountability for what you're doing.

I have learned a lot, over the years, from throwing myself on the sword in a polite way. What I mean by that is, whenever I can, I admit I made a mistake in not doing my job to the best of my ability. Once I do that, it's clear that I am committed to improving my own process and committed to being accountable for my own results. Now my contact is full of confidence, and I am much more likely to get the information I need.

I like to think I would have closed that deal my client lost. And I like to think you could, too. For both you and me, regardless of where we are in the selling cycle, the essential starting point would be accountability for our own actions.

If you are truly accountable, you will ask questions and you will encourage the prospect to ask questions. You will uncover the true reason a client feels that he or she does not want to meet with you (or, for that matter, buy from you). Once you know what that reason is, you are in a much better position to do something about it.

My parting message to you is this. If you lead with accountability during the prospecting phase of the sale, you will be in a position to lead with accountability throughout the entire sales process. On the other hand, if you don't lead the prospecting phase, you'll be following for the rest of the sales cycle. That would be a shame.

It is a proven fact that you can double your business buy becoming an expert in prospecting. I'm interested in hearing about your experiences as you implement this program. Please drop me a line at caquin@ gunpowderbusiness.com.

Be accountable. Take the lead. Break through. Have fun!

Happy hunting,
Christine Aquin Pope

Christine

APPENDIX A

A Real-Life Bulletproofing Example

I've provided you with different samples throughout the book, but I thought it would be helpful for you to see real-life example of Bulletproofing in action. Below are some of the tools I used to Bulletproof my team en route to successful campaign for one of my clients.

TACTIC 1: BASIC TRAINING AND RECONNAISSANCE

Please remember that you must not sound scripted when you make these calls. Below is the script that I provided for my EA to use to determine the right person to contact within the target organization. Note that it allows for flexibility.

Nancy, please ask for the executive assistant to the president. Ask her for help. If you get information from the receptionist, please verify it with the EA of the CEO.

Good morning/afternoon_____, this is Nancy Black, executive assistant to: Christine Aquin here at Software Innovation. I am hoping you can help direct me. I have been asked to set up an educational session with your senior management. I would like to know who at your company would be interested in learning about global best practices & compliance for Capital Project Execution (large construction projects).

I am preparing the invitations and I would like help in determining who best to invite from your company.

(Depending which type of company you call you might ask:)

Who would be responsible for project execution of large capital projects at your company?

Do you have a project execution team? Who is in charge of building the facilities?

We provide our customers with team/project communications for optimizing capital projects around the world.

For example, Fluor, one of the world's largest Engineering, Procurement,

---

and Construction companies, has deployed our best practices on over 100 plus projects in 25 countries around the world.

Project collaboration is one of the most important issues your company is facing and we would like to make sure you are included in this educational session.

We maintain offices in Houston and Calgary. The primary markets we service are the Engineering, Oil & Gas, Infrastructure, and Power and Utilities marketplaces. Some of our clients like Chevron, the world's second largest energy company, are also enjoying the benefits of our experience.

Let them give you a few names then ask for more: CEO, Senior Manager of Environmental Group, Senior Manager of Project Controls, VP of Engineering, SVP Project Execution and/or Operations, Head of Project Management and Best Practices.

Please try and get several names from each company and details about what their role involves. I will need names, titles, email addresses, and mailing addresses.

Below is a slightly different script that I used to track down the right person.

Hi Mary,

I am wondering if you can help direct me. I am Christine Aquin, executive assistant for (Mr. Springs, Tompkins, Sunderland, Logan) here at Coreworx. My directors have asked me to contact your company to arrange a senior discussion regarding best practices and methodologies for more efficient project execution.

Do you have a project execution team? Could you suggest the best person to meet with? Someone interested in reducing costs around large Capital projects or increasing the efficiencies or doing more work with less people? Project Manager?

We are the global leaders in project execution. We work in over 20 nations around the world with companies like Fluor, KBR, and Chevron—helping them to improve their ability to deliver projects on time and on budget.

My directors asked me to contact you because we work with all kinds of companies and yet we have never had a discussion with anyone at your company. We would like to set up an introductory meeting to share our experience and see if there might be some synergies with our companies down the road.Hi Mary,

I am wondering if you can help direct me. I am Christine Aquin, executive assistant for (Mr. Springs, Tompkins, Sunderland, Logan) here at Coreworx. My directors have asked me to contact your company to arrange a senior discussion regarding best practices and methodologies for more efficient project execution.

Do you have a project execution team? Could you suggest the best person to meet with? Someone interested in reducing costs around large Capital projects or increasing the efficiencies or doing more work with less people? Project Manager?

We are the global leaders in project execution. We work in over 20 nations around the world with companies like Fluor, KBR, and

Chevron—helping them to improve their ability to deliver projects on time and on budget.

My directors asked me to contact you because we work with all kinds of companies and yet we have never had a discussion with anyone at your company. We would like to set up an introductory meeting to share our experience and see if there might be some synergies with our companies down the road.

TACTIC 2: FIRST CONTACT

I generally prefer to use bullet-point notes rather than a script when I leave a voice mail message for a decision maker, because I think it sounds fresher. However, here is an example of a script that I provided for my assistant to use when she left messages. Note that she does not give her title. She also does not mention that she's calling from Software Innovations; this prevents us from being rerouted to IT. It's a small detail, but it allowed us to open some very big doors for our client.

Big smile!

Hi Mary, this is Nancy Black. My directors have asked me to contact your company to arrange a senior discussion regarding best practices and methodologies for more efficient project execution.

We would like to meet with your team interested in reducing costs around large capital projects.

We are the global leaders in project execution. We work in over 20 nations around the world and help companies to improve their ability to deliver projects on time and on budget. Companies like Fluor, KBR, and Chevron.

Our approach gives you a way to manage the detailed processes involved in large scale capital projects by providing audit trails that record project communication and transactions; making each member of a project team 100% accountable. When there is a delay or miscommunication, you will immediately know the source and be able to take action to remedy it.

We help around things like project hand over, commissioning, and implementing best practices for Engineering Interface Management and Action Tracking for Regulatory Affairs to reduce cost overruns on large capital projects.

I will send you a detailed e-mail with some client examples.

We would like to discuss your current approach to managing capital projects to determine if our solution could provide tremendous value for your organization. I can be reached at 555-555-5555.

Again, this is Nancy Black and my number is 555-555-5555.

Have a great day!

TACTIC 3: ELECTRONIC WARFARE

Here is the email that I used as a follow up to the voice mail message.

Dear _____,

According to a recent study by Independent Project Analysis Inc., in the last 20 years 14 of the industry's largest projects have experienced an average cost growth of 46%. On a $1 billion project, 46% amounts to $460 million. In today's market, companies that can effectively manage capital projects on schedule, within budget, and with operational excellence have a clear and sustainable competitive advantage.

Designed by engineers for firms engaged in complex capital projects similar to those in the oil, gas, and construction-engineering industries, Coreworx is purpose built enterprise software solution designed to optimize capital project execution allowing decentralized project teams to collaborate and communicate globally—anywhere and anytime. Our solutions are used by companies like Fluor and Chevron to strengthen their competitive position and mitigate project risks across a diverse portfolio of projects—and all have been able to clearly demonstrate cost savings, increased project value, and greater customer satisfaction.

"Fluor's investment in Projects Online, built on the Coreworx platform, provides our project teams with a tool that is designed specifically to support the unique collaboration and document control processes and requirements of our industry, resulting in improved project execution and reduced project risks." – Glenn Golkey (Vice President, Project Execution Services, Fluor Corporation)

Without sacrificing the ability to meet unique project needs, Coreworx enables standardization of best practices across the organization. It is easy to use and fast to roll out across multiple complex projects. Integrating easily to the major software packages, it provides efficient, secure access and allows controlled exchange of documentation to and from key participants of a project. Detailed audit trails and reporting functionality enable project teams to auditably manage project interfaces across any number of locations, suppliers, and subcontractors, resulting in 100% accountability. By eliminating confusion and lost data in the interface process, project timelines are preserved and post-project litigation can be pre-empted or greatly reduced.

Unlike project management software, Coreworx offers the full technical document management functionality required for engineering content. It is a project execution solution that performs the actual content creation and revision, along with the associated communication and collaboration.

Without consistent control, project risk accelerates and the potential for project delays, cost overruns, and other negative outcomes increases. If you would like to increase the speed in which projects are completed, improve project performance, standardize interface processes across all projects and rectify the critical issues that arise when managing large capital projects, then we have the solution that will unequivocally deliver.

We will be calling you shortly to arrange a brief meeting to better understand your concerns and to provide you with information on how Software Innovation's Coreworx solution suite can increase the success of your capital projects.

Yours Truly,

Nancy Black

And here's the case study which was sent as a PDF attachment to the email above.

COREWORX
Project Collaboration
CASE STUDY

CUSTOMER BUSINESS PROFILE:

Fluor provides world-class engineering, procurement, construction, operations, maintenance and project management services.

Fluor has a track record of outstanding dependability, expertise and safety in the global building services market.

EMPLOYEES: 30,000+

GEOGRAPHIES: Worldwide

COREWORX APPLICATIONS: Coreworx, Coreworx DMS

DEPLOYMENT SUMMARY

- 18,000+ Projects OnLineSM users worldwide

- Deployed on 100+ projects in 25 Countries

- 2,000+ Equipment Suppliers and Sub-contractors

BENEFITS

- Reduces client costs

- Streamlines project startup

- Improves project collaboration capability

- Mitigates risk

- Allows true global execution as project teams work together from diverse locations

- Enables project teams to rapidly and securely share information and documents with suppliers and subcontractors

- Provides audit trails to record project communication and transactions

- Reduces reproduction costs

- Eliminates expense and delivery time of courier packages

- Provides an efficient method for delivering electronic final deliverables at mechanical completion and start-up and commissioning

FLUOR'S ADVANTAGE

Fluor has a track record of outstanding dependability, expertise and safety in the global building services market. Over the past century, customers have relied on Fluor to develop, execute, and maintain capital projects on schedule, within budget, and with operational excellence. In today's competitive marketplace, the pressures of globalization and worksharing along with the need to lower costs and mitigate project risk led Fluor to develop an integrated execution platform to help maintain a competitive edge. The MasterPlant® suite helps Fluor streamline work and focus on providing customers with informed solutions. Coreworx forms the heart of Fluor's web-enabled collaboration and document management capability within the MasterPlant suite.

FLUOR AND COREWORX

Fluor selected technology from Software Innovation to deliver on its vision of an integrated project collaboration toolset to support the demanding requirements of the most complex projects in the world as well as smaller projects and studies. Internally branded Projects OnLine, this solution provides Fluor with a range of functionality designed to support the collaboration and document control processes involved in executing large capital projects as well as smaller projects.

The key components of the solution as delivered to Fluor include a web collaboration suite (Coreworx) and an embedded project document management system (Coreworx DMS). Together, these components provide Fluor with the ability to securely manage engineering, supplier, sub-contractor, and construction documentation on projects around the globe.

Beginning with a pilot project in 2002 Projects OnLine has seen a world class pace of implementation across the Fluor organization, rapidly scaling up to meet demand. As of December 2004, the system boasts a user base in excess of 13,000 users across more than 65 projects in 25 countries. This still-growing user base now conducts more than 350,000 document transactions per month, underscoring the scalability and reliability of the solution

SECURE GLOBAL WORKSHARING

By providing this secure global worksharing environment for Fluor, the Coreworx solution enables the project staff including clients, partners, construction and suppliers to collaborate and communicate effectively by providing access to documents, drawings and work packages for each project. The robust security architecture enables Fluor to share key files with suppliers and subcontractors around the world as needed without compromising security. More than 1.5 million file transactions occurred in Projects OnLine in 2004 and the solution continues to expand.

The web-based thin-client technology of Coreworx minimizes training requirements and the solution can be accessed from anywhere in the world with an internet connection, Microsoft Internet Explorer, and authorized access rights. The integrated viewer / red-line tool supports numerous file formats making it possible to open, view, annotate, and print files, including drawing files, without the native application.

PROJECTS ONLINE AND COREWORX IN ACTION

The power delivered by the Projects OnLine solution has been key in the execution of a major oil and gas development project in northeast Russia. The project area is comprised of three major oilfields with total recoverable reserves estimated at over 2 billion barrels of oil (307 million tons) and over 17 trillion cubic feet of natural gas (485 billion cubic meters). Capital investment in this project could reach US $12 billion, making it the largest foreign direct investment in Russia. Project benefits to Russia include direct revenues, estimated at US$40 billion, improvement of infrastructure, and the use of Russian sub-contractors and equipment suppliers.

Fluor was chosen by the owner/operator consortium in mid-2003 to provide construction management services for the project. Under this contract Fluor manages several large Russian contractors constructing an onshore oil and gas processing facility and well-pad infrastructure near the field. In early 2004 Fluor was awarded a second contract to provide engineering and procurement services in association with selected Russian Design Institutes.

Fluor's experience in executing complex global projects married with the power of Projects OnLine have significantly minimized the logistical challenges of project execution involving multiple companies with offices around the world. Over 750 project members are led by a core team in the United States with more than 180 international users participate from locations in Russia, Korea, India and Japan.

A large amount of information is being managed through Projects OnLine for this project, with current document count close to 60,000, and 250,000 + related files totalling 140 gigabytes of data, and including:

- 26,000 Engineering / Design Documents

- 24,500 Supplier Documents

- 800 Project Execution Documents (Conference

Notes, Project Procedures Manual, Contract Information, etc.)

- 4,000 Reference Documents

- 175 Interface Documents

- 1,200 Subcontractor documents

- 2,700 Russian Code Documents

BENEFITS OF COREWORX TO THE PROJECT

Projects OnLine provides the means to manage and distribute documentation electronically as well as giving the project team a central, shared communication and collaboration tool accessible regardless of location. Electronic distribution has provided the latest information rapidly and efficiently, allowing the project to eliminate entirely the usual international courier costs and has reduced overall reproduction costs as well as providing the ability to execute in a 24/7 environment.

The tight integration between the project portal and the document management database is a key factor in mitigating risk by insuring all users access one official, revision controlled version of a document or drawing coming from the master document database. This functionality eliminates the need to manage multiple copies of files in disparate locations. From a user's perspective, the interface to the document management archives is seamless, and enables users with various access levels and minimal technical sophistication to share documents and work packages with the assurance that the correct and latest revision is being employed. The construction teams in particular have benefited from the ability to access the most recent revised information immediately after issue. Traditional paper distribution by courier service would average 7 days for delivery to this remote construction site. Due to weather conditions, construction has less than 60 working days per year making electronic drawing access imperative.

The integrated supplier / sub-contractor interface in Projects OnLine has provided an efficient, secure, access controlled exchange of documentation to and from these key participants of the project. Utilizing this area of the system from the bid / proposal stage through the exchange of technical documentation has reduced the recycle time between supplier and project team during critical periods of engineering and design.

CHALLENGES

Three primary areas of challenge stand out on this and other projects: resolving 3rd party firewall / IT issues, providing acceptable band-width/ connectivity, and driving work process change.

A proactive approach at project start-up minimizes potential road blocks. Early interaction between IT organizations generally resolves firewall and access issues. Providing acceptable band/width and connectivity to remote areas may present a more difficult challenge, however, the use of satellite links, and dedicated land lines, among other solutions, are beginning to be acknowledged as a basic service for most facilities today and planned for early on. The use of Projects OnLine on this project has proved the slowest connectivity to a remote construction site is faster than the most rapid courier service. Work process changes for the end user may be met with resistance, with some users adapting more quickly than others. Projects OnLine was developed to provide simple, easy access to information, however a key factor to acceptance has been providing short, 1 hour maximum, group training sessions for task force teams. This effort provides users with a basic understanding of the system and facilitates acceptance and use.

THE ROAD AHEAD

Projects OnLine, powered by the Coreworx technology from Software Innovation, provides a key set of features and functions that support Fluor best practices and help Fluor to maintain a competitive edge in its business. By providing an integrated solution that encompasses collaboration, document management and other key functionalities, Coreworx is helping Fluor position itself for continued growth while maintaining its high standards for quality, risk management and project safety.

ABOUT FLUOR

Fluor provides services on a global basis in the fields of engineering, procurement, construction, operations, maintenance and project management. Headquartered in Aliso Viejo, California, Fluor is a FORTUNE 500 company with revenues of nearly $9 billion in 2003. For more information, visit www.fluor.com.

ABOUT SOFTWARE INNOVATION

Software Innovation provides web-based project collaboration software, Coreworx, which enables the management of and collaboration on large capital projects. Coreworx helps engineering firms and owner/operators automate their best practices and improve project performance, resulting in reduced risk, improved project control, more rapid project completion, and significant cost savings. For more information, visit www.softinn.com.

www.softinn.com

Kitchener: 22 Frederick Street, Suite 800, Kitchener, Ontario, Canada Tel: 519.772.3181 Fax: 519.772.3182 Toll-free: 1-888-SOFTINN

Houston: 1330 Post Oak Blvd., Suite 1600, Houston, Texas, USA Tel:

TACTIC 4: VOICE-TO-VOICE COMBAT

Here are the notes I used to jog my memory as I engaged in voice-to-voice combat with the target organizations.

What we offer at Coreworx is a process that integrates all the systems that you already have in place for managing your capital projects to make them more effective. We help systems interact with each other. Suppliers, owners, and vendors all have different systems and large investments in each system. Systems like SAP, Open Text, and Documentum. These systems are very costly and very expensive to customize.

Examples of how we help:

At AMEC they have people who manually input project transmittals. Sometimes they are weeks behind starting a project simply because they don't have the resources for inputting the data. We have a way to turn three weeks of manual inputting into three days.

Bechtel has invested a great deal of resources into documentum. They have teams of people that build custom applications for hundreds of projects-customized workflow--very costly. Our clients can customize without programming. One administrative person can replace 15 to 20 application people.

At AMEC, project teams struggle on several other fronts. Currently their information resides in two different systems. One is a document repository, and the other is a web-based portal. Project teams cannot cur-

---

rently access working documents without leaving one environment and entering the other one. This is very tough on remote projects as well as very tedious in general. Document version control is still a big problem for many of our clients. Our service solves all that.

We work with companies like Fluor and Chevron. Our approach gives you a way to manage the detailed processes involved in large scale capital projects by providing audit trails that record project communication and transactions, making each member of a project team 100% accountable. When there is a delay or miscommunication you will immediately know the source and be able to take action to remedy it.

Further, we help leverage the ease of migration to SharePoint and newer technologies while allowing faster and more automated customization. Clients can better service their customer by offering more flexibility.

We help around things like project hand over and commissioning, and implementing best practices for Engineering Interface Management and Action Tracking for Regulatory Affairs to reduce cost overruns on large capital projects.

We would like to discuss your current approach to managing capital projects to determine if our solution could provide value for your organization.

Our roots are in Norway, starting with the oil industry over there, have grown into Houston, and are now in Calgary. In Calgary our solutions are used at CNRL's Horizon Project and on Opti/Nexen's Long Lake project.

Primavera is primarily a Project Management solution.

Coreworx is primarily a Project Execution solution.

What is the difference? Project Management is typically about planning, scheduling, and managing the personnel, resources, and costs associated with a project. Project Execution is about performing the actual content creation and revision, along with the associated communication and collaboration. The actual processes, documents/drawings, and so on within Coreworx may be referred to as milestones or deliverables on a Gantt chart within Primavera, for instance.

APPENDIX B

Dressing for Clout, Confidence, and Credibility

By Karen Brunger

"Nothing succeeds like the appearance of success."
~ RICHARD FEYNMAN

You've scheduled the meeting. You've done your research and prepared for the meeting. You've mapped out all the right tactics and strategies for the meeting. Now for the big question: what do you wear to the meeting?

It's time to don your shining armour—or, at any rate, its modern-day equivalent for the business battlefield. Soldiers who don't take the time to plan and choose their uniforms with care and consideration risk sabotaging themselves on the field of battle.

Think about it. You've worked so hard and so long to set yourself up for success at this meeting. Doesn't it make sense to invest just a little more time so you can make the right wardrobe choices? Failing to invest that time really can cost you the deal!

FOUR LEVELS OF BUSINESS DRESS

There are four levels of dress for business, each relatively easy to spot:

Level One: Formal Corporate
Level Two: Business
Level Three: Business Casual
Level Four: Casual Business

As a matter of strategy, I strongly recommend that you choose Formal Corporate for the first meeting with any prospective client. As a salesperson, you generally cannot make a mistake by dressing a level or two above the style of the prospect...but you can certainly lose the deal by dressing a level or two below the prospect.

LEVEL ONE

Let's look more closely, then, at Level One, which is what I would suggest for all initial meetings and for any high-level meetings, as well. At Level One, your image has absolute power, authority, and credibility. This look is appropriate for any situation where a high level of trust, reliability, and stability is required.

The Suit

A sharp-looking suit is the easiest and most effective way to portray power and authority. The most formal corporate suit is dark, cold-based colour, and neutral, which means navy blue or charcoal. Black may seem like a safe choice, but it can present problems, as it can look like an evening suit.

The suit should be made of very fine wool; I usually look for wool that's rated at least "Super 100."(The number indicates the number of fibres per inch.) "Super 120" looks even more elegant and refined. Invest in the best quality suit you can afford. I usually recommend that your best suit cost 1 percent of your gross annual income.

The most formal suit is solid in colour, but a pinstripe pattern is also acceptable at this level. Beware: the more obvious the pattern, the less professional the image.

The style of the suit should be classic and tailored. For women, a skirt is more formal than trousers. It should be knee-length, with straight, sharp lines.

The Shirt

The higher the contrast between the shirt and the suit, the more professional and formal the effect will be. A white shirt is the most formal. I suggest choosing a shade that complements your personal colouring, perhaps ice white, soft white, ivory, or cream.

Guidelines for men:

Choose shirts in fine cotton. Any topstitching should be close to the edge, and should have a refined look.

Guidelines for women:

You face more of a challenge in getting the right top to wear under a suit. While a man has a tie to fill in the collar, you don't have this option. If you choose a collared shirt, you need to make sure that the collar of the top does not conflict with the collar of the jacket. You could also choose a high-neck shell. Keep in mind that the lower your neckline, the less professional your impression. It never ceases to amaze me how often corporate women who are trying for Level One show off their cleavage. This is not where you want the focus to go.

The Tie (Men Only)

The most formal colours for a tie are variations of gray, blue, gold, and red. The best formal patterns include solids, repeating diagonal lines, foulard (a repeating geometric pattern), and pin-dot.

Pay attention to your tie length! For a conservative image, the tip of your tie should come to the top of your belt buckle. If you require a more creative, progressive image, the tip of your tie could come ¼ inch below your belt buckle.

Use a tie-knot in proportion to your build. If you have a narrow face or a slim build, you could use a 4-in-hand. If your face and build is average, you could use the Half Windsor. If you have more fullness in your face and build, you could use the Full Windsor. If any of this sounds unfamiliar, check out this website: www.tie-a-tie.net for more information.

The Pocket Square (Men Only)

A white linen pocket square is the most formal choice. If you want to show some flair and creativity, you can go with coloured silk. The pocket square should match a colour in the shirt or tie.

The way the pocket square is folded can make a big difference. The most formal folds are straight, triangle, and petal. (The puff and casual folds are best reserved for less formal situations.) Confused? Take a look at www.wikihow.com/Fold-a-Pocket-Square for details.

Shoes

Make sure your shoes are immaculate and in good condition. They should be made of leather and reflect a classic, yet updated, style.

Guidelines for men:

An Oxford (lace-up) shoe sends the most formal message; it should look refined and elegant rather than rustic and chunky. Black shoes are safest for projecting the formal corporate image.

Guidelines for women:

A pump with a closed toe and a medium height closed heel is the most formal choice. Important: the shoe should match or be darker than your hemline.

The Belt

The belt should match your shoes. A good corporate belt is made of smooth leather and features a classic (not distracting) buckle. Men: if you wear suspenders, a belt is not necessary.

Hosiery

Guidelines for men:

Match your socks to your trousers. It's not a faux pas to match the shoes, but it's not the best image. Executive length socks, which cover the calves, ensure we won't see your hairy leg when you sit and cross your legs.

Guidelines for women:

Wear sheer hose to match your skin colour.

Jewellery

The jewellery with the strongest professional image is made of gold (yellow or white) or platinum. Jewellery should be classic, simple, and moderate in size. Both men and women can wear a watch, plus one ring per hand. Men can wear a tie clip and collar pin. Women can wear stud earrings.

The Briefcase

The narrower your briefcase, the higher your perceived status. Choose good quality leather. Women should not carry a handbag and briefcase at the same time.

The Pen

When you pull out your pen, it must not be an 89-cent plastic ballpoint! The pen doesn't have to be extremely expensive (although that certainly doesn't hurt), but it should look elegant. The pen must be made of metal.

Eyewear

Wire frames are professional looking, whereas plastic frames tend to look sporty or casual. Use non-reflective and non-tinted lenses. Make sure your eyewear is updated and gives you the competitive edge in terms of appearance. The eyewear you choose can make you look outdated and passé...or credible and savvy.

Hair

For both sexes, formal hair styles are sleek and controlled. Hair that touches the shoulder projects a more casual image.

Guidelines for men:

It's generally best if you're clean-shaven, as facial hair can sabotage you. (Come to think of it, this advice applies to women as well. Women who have reached menopausal years often need to watch for hair coming out of the chin.) If there is obvious hair in places that could be distracting, such as your nose and ears, this should be clipped. I sometimes see a man who has a beautiful short haircut, but who also has tufts of hair climbing up out of the back of his shirt and onto his neck. Ugh.

Guidelines for women:

As a general rule, slightly shorter is best for Level One. Go to a reputable hair stylist on a regular basis; you want your hair style to be current and flattering. Of course, your hair should be neat, clean, and in good condition. If you colour your hair, bear in mind that natural colours are going to be perceived as more credible than unnatural ones. Leave the fuchsia hair for your personal time. Make sure your hair colour harmonizes with your natural colouring. You will send a conflicting message if your hair is warm, your skin tone and eyes are cool. If you have not had a personal colour analysis with a professional, you may want to consider this before investing in a change in hair colour.

Makeup

Men should not wear makeup.

For women, the general rule is that all makeup should be neutral in tone and natural-looking. There is, however, an important exception to this rule: women who wear red lipstick get listened to more than women who wear any other colour. Of course, you must make sure that the shade of red you choose, whether it's cherry red, soft red, scarlet, or brick, harmonizes with and complements your natural colouring.

I recommend that women have a makeup lesson once a year to keep their look fresh and updated.

Nails

Having a manicure every week can keep your nails attractive and in good condition. (A pedicure once a month is also a good idea.) You don't want hangnails, broken nails, ragged cuticles, or chipped polish. For a formal corporate look, a clear polish or French manicure is appropriate for women.

Teeth

A nice white smile says success. A consultation with a cosmetic dentist can help you decide whether there is work to be done.

Cleaning your teeth on a regular basis helps keep your teeth healthy and your breath fresh. Here are my top five tips to assist with fresh breath, which is an absolute must in any professional setting, such as a sales meeting:

- Drink water with lemon—the lemon helps kill bacteria.
- Eat dark green leafy foods, such as parsley.
- Eat crispy foods such as celery and carrot sticks. (They act as an abrasive on the gums.)
- Avoid dairy foods before the meeting.
- Use an oral breath strip.

Grooming and Hygiene

Shower and use a deodorant. Avoid fragrance in business, as it can be distracting, unprofessional, and inconsiderate. Many people are allergic to fragrance.

ALTERNATE LEVELS

Once you have left a great first impression at the first meeting, you may choose to adopt one of the other levels of professional business dress. Here's a brief summary of each.

Level Two: Business

This look is appropriate for general business, or where some creativity or individuality is desired. There is flexibility in styles, colours, and patterns of the suit, shirt, and tie.

Level Three: Business Casual

This look may work if your meeting is at a sporting event. A jacket is still worn, but it's not part of a matched suit. Shoes are more casual—a loafer or walking shoe.

Level Four: Casual Business

This is an extremely casual look for business. It is "sans jacket"—just a shirt and trousers or (for women) an appropriate top and skirt.

PUTTING IT ALL TOGETHER

"Who you are speaks so loudly I can't hear what you say."
~RALPH WALDO EMERSON

Your image speaks powerfully for you—or against you—before you even open your mouth! Consider the following true story.

Paul's Story

As the president and owner of a business specializing in information technology, Paul sells his products to presidents of Fortune 500 companies. One CEO told Paul that he should see an image consultant, as he was sabotaging his own business. Paul became my client.

Paul had not factored his own image into the product promotion equation. As a result, his image was uncoordinated, unprofessional, and unflattering. His clothes were selected with no consideration for colour, fabric, or appropriateness.

Working together, we quickly discarded about 95 percent of his wardrobe. Then we introduced clothes that would allow him to be comfortable, appropriate, and credible, not only for his important meetings, but in all facets of his life. The colours, fabrics, and styles we chose suited his body type, colouring, and personality.

A month after I completed my work with Paul, I received a telephone call from him. He was almost speechless, he was so overcome with emotion. He said, "I can't begin to tell you the difference that this has made in my life." He reported that his income had tripled, and members of his staff were now treating him with much more respect. As if that weren't enough, women were approaching him socially!

Once you make the choices that allow your image to enhance your professional success, great things really do begin to happen!

ABOUT KAREN BRUNGER

Karen Brunger is Director of the International Image Institute Inc. and Past-President of the Association of Image Consultants International. Karen is a recipient of the International Award of Excellence in Image Consulting.

As a trainer, Karen has presented on five continents, and her image systems and products are currently used in over 60 countries. Karen is a co-author of Executive Image Power and a contributing writer to B Magazine. Karen also appears regularly as a guest expert in the media.

With over twenty-five years of experience as an image consultant, Karen has optimized the appearance, behaviour, and communications of over 2,000 individuals, helping to ensure they achieve more of their own potential.

Contact Karen Brunger:

www.imageinstitute.com

karenbrunger@imageinstitute.com

PRAISE FOR KAREN BRUNGER

"Thank you for the truly inspiring wealth of information you shared with us at the AICI conference in Singapore. What a great impact your workshop had on me. I loved every minute of it." ~ Kimberley Bux

"Karen is warm, authentic, and powerful. She empowers me to be me." ~ Lois Ferguson, President, Malibu Consulting International – Toronto, Ontario

APPENDIX C

Excerpted from the forthcoming book

Gunpowderbusiness: True Sales Turnarounds from the Front Lines

A True Story from the Front Lines

Master sales coach Gregory Cleary was my sales manager at Peak Performance Training, Brian Tracy's sales training organization. Greg now runs a very successful sales coaching business of his own. Action Learning trains sales professionals all over North America. In a recent conversation, I asked Gregory to share a story about a salesperson he had coached to a big turnaround. Here's what he shared from the front lines.

At Action Learning, we work intensely with salespeople on the critical question: "What are you going to do that makes you different from all the other people out there who you're competing against?" You can't be the same; you must stand out from the crowd. We review everything. For some guys, we say, "Get some spectacles, you need to look older and more experienced." I tell them, "You know what? It's bad out there. I don't care if everyone in the street is wearing polo shirts and khaki pants. You are going to wear a tie. You are going to be one level above everyone else." And that means a lot more than wardrobe, by the way. We work out every single aspect of the sales process, including how they get appointments, how they research customers, and how they begin a meeting. They all have to be a level above the rest of the field. For instance, if you see the fish up on the wall and you say, "Oh, are you a fisherman?"—that's a major sin in my book. You should know that every single salesperson who has walked in that office before you has asked that same question. It's your responsibility to bring the game to the next level.

A prime example of someone who fully embraces this idea is Joe Van-Hoorn. When I first met Joe, he was working his butt off for an industrial supply company. He was driving a ten-year-old car, his salary was capped at

$50,000 per year, and I could tell he was unhappy with his income situation. We had a long talk about that; I remember Joe telling me that he felt like he was giving diamonds to a pawn shop at that job. After all, he was working hard and still struggling to support his wife and five kids. From the moment we started working together, he was hungry to change his world.

So he made a tough decision. He decided to leave the steady job, the job where his income potential was capped, and move on to a situation where he had unlimited income potential. Taking the new job was a big risk, because he had to go from field sales to inside sales, but it was a risk he felt he had to take. He just didn't like the place he had landed in his life.

Now he sells components to heating, ventilation, and air conditioning contractors, and he's completely turned his career around; he's just been blowing the doors off. The other day, he and I were reminiscing and looking back at the goals he set for himself. In 2006, his goal was $1.5 million, and his stretch goal was $1.8 million. In 2009 he did about $4 million, and his goal for next year is $6 million. He makes about 5 percent commission, so if you do the math—he went from earning fifty grand a year to earning two hundred grand a year. What's more, he works mostly from home now, which is a much better lifestyle for him, and he's enjoying a lot more time with his kids.

What changed? Joe became fearless. He committed to differentiating himself from the competition and he practiced his techniques and strategies endlessly. He wanted new things to try, which is very different from the attitude a lot of salespeople bring to the coaching process. He would listen to every instruction I gave him, practice it, and implement it with total faith. Now, I want to emphasize that you really do have to practice a lot to become fearless. We have a saying in my industry: **competence breeds confidence.** In fact, that's a big part of what we do at

Action Learning: we get salespeople to practice a new strategy until they feel completely committed to it.

PRACTICE MAKES PERFECT

For example, I make every single one of the people I coach create a brand-new introduction. This is the answer to the question, "What can you tell me about what you do?" That's what you want to lead a meeting with, of course, whether a prospect poses the question or not. You must have a good introduction, one that makes you stand out from the competition! So I always critique introductions relentlessly.

Once someone nails the introduction, I make that person practice it over and over and over again—until he or she is fully competent at delivering it. The big thing salespeople have to remember here is that you can't just practice the words; you also have to practice the emotion as you deliver the introduction. I keep hounding people until they can tell me their whole story with both the right words and the right music. Your clients want to know "What's in it for me?" You have to be able to tell me that concisely and in an emotionally compelling way, and what you say has to pass the "so what" test.

When we start this process, most people answer the question "What do you do?" with something like this: "Well, we've been around for 100 years and we have 50,000 square feet..." You know, so what? That just doesn't cut the mustard. When people ask me "What do you do?" I know I don't want to say, "Actually, I've been doing this for 25 years. I do sales coaching and sales training, and customer service. I can hire some salespeople for you, and I can ride along on sales calls." Why don't I want to say that? Because everyone else can say, "So what? I do that too." Instead, my answer goes like this: "I help companies capture new businesses faster than they ever thought possible, but with no rejection in the sales process." That stops the other person cold! Now the person I'm talking to is curious: "How do you do that?" This is the point at which I can talk about all the ways I do what I do—once I've gotten the person to ask a question. That's the way you make your introduction look and sound different from everyone else's. I go through that process with everyone I coach, including Joe.

STANDING OUT FROM THE CROWD

Joe started his new job as an inside salesperson, but he quickly earned a spot as one of the field reps. Every single one of Joe's accounts loves him. He's got a great sense of humor, which helps him to stand out. I'll give you an example of what I mean. Last week, he was launching a new territory, and part of his campaign will be familiar to people who have read this book. He does a nine-touch campaign before he reaches the person voice-to-voice, meaning he sends his prospects nine promotional mailing pieces. (This is the "bombing the beach" strategy.)

I happened to be listening in on a follow-up call Joe was making to one of these prospects; he had the call on speakerphone so I could listen in.

Joe: "I'm calling for two reasons. One is to make sure you are receiving the promotional pieces I'm sending out."

The guy on the other end of the line says, "Yeah, we're getting those."

Joe says, "Okay, great. The other reason I'm calling is to see what you thought of them."

The prospect says, "I thought they were kind of cute."

Joe says, "Cute? Did you say cute? Okay, hold on for a second."

And Joe puts the phone to his chest, and screams out, "Hey! Who sent the cute stuff out? I said masculine! Masculine to these HVAC contractors!"

He comes back on the phone and says, "I'm so sorry about that."

And of course, the guy on the phone is laughing and Joe gets the appointment. He does that kind of stuff all day, every day. And the difference between what he's doing now and what he was doing five years ago is that he's channeling his entire personality into the job, and he's doing it with complete positive expectation.

Just recently, Joe told me about a big customer he had inherited from another representative. He was supposed to call the key person at this account. We all know it's a little awkward to call someone up and say, "Hi, I'm your new rep; I'm taking over." At the time he got this new account, I had been working with Joe on the concept of differentiating himself from other salespeople. So, rather than calling up the new account, he walked into the lobby of the company, completely unannounced, and asked to see the manager who was supposed to be his contact. He gets to the manager, introduces himself, and the manager says, "What do you want?"

Joe says, "Well, I was in a poker game last night at our company, and I won your account."

Of course, the manager is astonished. He says, "You did what?"

Joe says, "Yeah, I won your account last night in the poker game, so I just wanted to come by and say hello." And the manager starts cracking up.

That's something Joe definitely would not have done five years ago. Now that he understands the importance of being different and practicing his techniques, he is confident enough to be out there connecting with people in a fun way, bringing his own energy and humor to the entire sales process. He can do that because he is fully prepared in what he's doing and you can be too!

Another great example of the way Joe brings his game to the next level is the question he asks at the opening of a meeting. I made him practice a specific opening question for face-to-face meetings with new prospects. Now, why did I make him practice that question? Because his job is to look, sound, and act differently than all the other salespeople he's competing with. That's his responsibility. So here's the opening question he uses now: "I'm just curious, why'd you decide to set the time aside to meet with me today?"

A lot of salespeople shy away from that one, because it seems to give the prospect the opportunity to say, "Hey, wait a minute—why did I agree to meet with you? What am I doing here?" But Joe has had great results with the question. Of course, it's one that has to be asked with full commitment and a lot of confidence. Sometimes the answer Joe gets by asking this question at the beginning of the meeting takes him right to the heart of sale: "Well, my current vendor just dropped the ball again." That's good to know! Or: "I just got another price increase." Wouldn't you rather find out about that at the beginning of the discussion? Or maybe he'll hear: "You know what? I agreed to meet with you because you had a lot of energy and you are just plain persistent. I liked your style." That's great, you want to know what got you in the door. Or he might hear: "I really liked that multi-piece mailing you guys sent, and I wanted to see whether we had a match here." Now he has a place to begin the discussion: "That's great to hear! Which piece of that mailing was the most interesting to you?" And he's up and running.

Right now, I think Joe would be successful in whatever industry he chose, but I don't think he could have reached that point without making a personal commitment to become who he is now. He had to have a moment of decision. When Joe decided to transition out of the $50,000-a-year job that was the moment he started creating his own spin. He started putting his own humor and personality into his career, and that was the beginning of his success. He's made himself his own masterpiece. He's reached the point where he can go to any city with the assignment of opening up a new territory, and have the complete expectation that he's going to meet everyone he needs to meet to make that happen and to secure all the commitments that support his goal. Once he accepts a goal like that, he's completely focused: "Give me the phone book." That's all he needs. He knows he can get an appointment with just about anyone.

Contact Gregory Cleary: www.actionlearning.biz

Christine Aquin Pope

Ignite your sales

www.gunpowderbusiness.com